RESORT STYLE

RESORT STYLE
SPACES OF CELEBRATION

ROGER THOMAS

With Jonah Lehrer

Foreword by
Cindy Allen

Essay by
Christopher Knight

Wynn Resorts

RIZZOLI
NEW YORK

New York Paris London Milan

This book is dedicated to my dear husband, Arthur, who insisted I do it, and to our talented daughter, Drew Thomas, for whom it was done.

TABLE OF CONTENTS

RULES...
WHAT RULES?!

by Cindy Allen

I am penning this (love) note, having just returned from a whirlwind business trip to Las Vegas, and because I only stay at the Wynn or Encore, Roger Thomas and his dazzling genius inspire me everywhere. Just entering Encore's all-red reception, greeted with oversize silk chrysanthemums (and dragonflies), and a triple-tiered ruby-red chandelier to boot, is stimulating and welcoming like a hug! It was actually early in my career as editor in chief, some two decades ago, when we first met. Just like it was yesterday, I recall encountering the dashing and debonaire Roger on that Vegas convention center floor. Checking each other wearing matching purple attire and eyewear—hey, it was very trendy then!—we became fast design friends, and never looked back.

At that time, Roger was smack in the middle of his four-decade-long partnership with casino mogul Steve Wynn, who has been his sole client since 1980. For his exceptional, super-engaged patron—whom he likens to a modern-day Medici—Roger has designed six resort hotels in Las Vegas, three in Macau, and most recently, Wynn's first East Coast property, Encore Boston Harbor. For any designer, Steve is the client one could only dream about, and this symbiotic, once-in-a-lifetime collaboration could best be described as remarkable! Together, they've revolutionized casino design by daring to break the rules, throw out those conventional ideas, and embrace innovative, original thinking. The result? Some of the most breathtaking hospitality interiors of our generation. This daring dynamic duo not only breathed fresh life into Sin City, reinvigorating the whole town, but also reimagined the contemporary resort casino, using design to achieve a dazzling new paradigm in luxury accommodations, amenities, and services. How many can put that on their CV?!

One may ask, what rules were tossed to the wind? Their initial groundbreaking move was to focus the design more on elevating the guest experience and less on maximizing casino revenue, lavishing the kind of creative attention and budget on a resort's suites, restaurants, entertainment venues, and retail boutiques that was traditionally reserved for its money-making gaming facilities. It was a risky business plan that paid off big and changed Las Vegas resort design and construction forever. By the time they opened the Bellagio in 1998, all the hallmarks of Roger's trailblazing programs were in place: interiors flooded with natural light (a former no-no); generous public spaces that maintain a sense of intimacy (no matter how grand); fabulous custom furnishings, finishes, and materials that rival those found in the finest European and Asian hotels (all authentic, nothing faux or fake here); and prioritizing indoor-outdoor environments, so that every restaurant, lounge, or meeting room boasts its own terrace, garden, or lagoon-side patio (can you say aaah?). When Roger toured me through the first in-hotel art galleries—filled with blue-chip masterpieces both historic and contemporary—I was completely stunned. And the luxury villas, also a first at the time, were so darn chic, one would never want to leave (and I suppose that was the point).

Roger went on refining and polishing his maverick craft, bringing it to the peak of perfection at the Wynn and the Encore, both wonderlands of extraordinary, going-for-broke opulence. Take the atrium at the Wynn, a fantasy landscape of towering ficus trees growing out of multicolor flower beds. What became a wowza moment—scores of two-foot-diameter floral balls suspended from the branches like oversize Christmas ornaments—was actually a late addition. Steve felt the upper reaches of the space lacked animation and Roger, remembering small Japanese silk-covered spheres he'd seen as a child at Gump's San Francisco, had them recreated on a bigger scale with blossoms. "Instant intimacy, delight, and surprise," he says. "They became an icon of the resort." And they continue to be an Instagram sensation today! I also adore the gorgeous mosaic floors Roger uses on both properties—brighter, more colorful versions of the ones he first used at the Bellagio. At the Wynn, he created gobsmacking oversize floral designs by painstakingly inlaying the marble floors with vibrant glass tesserae—"costly and difficult," he points out, "but the results were amazing." My personal fave? The giant mosaic butterflies that flit underfoot everywhere at Encore.

In another pioneering move, Roger invited many renowned designers to create custom restaurant and retail spaces, cameo appearances that "add contrast and texture to the experience," as he says. I marvel at the superb collaborations he's undertaken with celebrated designer Vicente Wolf over the years, particularly their first project—the SW Steakhouse, located beside the Wynn's Lake of Dreams—a room so enduringly elegant that Roger has had to do nothing more than refresh its soft finishes now and then.

Which brings me to one of Roger's most invaluable roles, that of the fully engaged mentor, generous with his time, erudition, and expertise. Many stellar careers have begun under his guiding hand at either Wynn Design & Development (WD&D) or the Roger Thomas Collection. One recent graduate of this rich learning environment is Alex Woogmaster, who founded his own hospitality and residential design studio in 2019 after almost a decade at WD&D. Alex got to see up-close just how Roger and Steve conjured their phenomenal resorts. "Roger envisions complete spaces before the project even begins, so he could paint verbal pictures for Steve at a rapid, improvisational level," Alex reports. "I never thought about it like this before, but it was almost like watching live jazz performed. Roger's vocabulary shifts between 'Designer French' and 'Society English'—Steve called this encyclopedic rolodex of design terminologies 'Gorgeois,' (rhymes with 'bourgeois'), which I think he considered fictitious but welcomed with chuckling respect." For this young designer-on-the-rise, those informative years proved a design masterclass with Roger at the helm graciously sharing those tools of the trade, and putting into practice his deep knowledge on the history of all the decorative arts creating one-of-a-kind hospitality spaces that everyone wants be in . . . and be seen in.

Which brings me back full circle to our first introduction. As an editor, I am always hunting for unique voices that will delight and surprise—yes, break those rules!—and set the pace for others moving forward. I knew I was meeting Vegas royalty strolling that convention floor together (there were adoring fans everywhere), but his wildly varied manufacturer collaborations were most impressive; furniture, fabric, wall covering, lighting, carpet, kitchen and bath, accessories, and hardware, just to name a few. The guy's prolific! (No one can turn a hand sketch into wall covering or reinvent a tassel like Roger!) That memorable day was the beginning of our enduring professional and personal story. In 2015, it was my honor to induct Roger into *Interior Design*'s Hall of Fame—our industry's Oscars—and witness the entire community on their feet celebrating his enormous contribution. Since then, I have continued to admire, publish, and cheer his design brilliance, and I suspect I will want to be part of Roger's magical world for many more years to come.

INVENTING A NEW LANGUAGE FOR CASINO RESORTS

by Roger Thomas

I've been designing hotel casinos for more than forty years. During that time, one of my favorite experiences has always been speaking to students. I love sharing my story, explaining the ideas behind my interiors, discussing how they came to be. This book is that discussion illustrated.

I always start by saying that I have the best job possible. That job is to make my own dreams—the designs I imagine in my sketchbook—come true. But that doesn't mean it has always been easy. That's because I didn't just want to design casinos—I wanted to create a new kind of interior, which required the invention of a unique design language. There are plenty of pretty spaces. But I dreamed of creating spaces that had never been seen before. I wanted people to walk into my rooms and gasp. I wanted to make them feel feelings that they'd never imagined experiencing in a Las Vegas resort.

I wish there had been a book like this when I was a young designer, struggling to find my own visual vocabulary. What I tell those students is that they can't be afraid to take risks and break rules. After all, if you're not taking risks, if you're not flirting with failure, then you're creating something we've seen before. And why bother doing that? It's a pity to spend an extraordinary amount of money and time designing a space that's not original. That isn't memorable. That doesn't contain elements of surprise and mystery and wonder.

One of my favorite Steve Wynn stories features Waylon Jennings. At the time, Wynn owned the Golden Nugget, and Jennings was one of his biggest performers. He took Waylon to see a young country star. When Waylon and Steve went backstage, the young singer started flattering Waylon, telling him he was a huge fan, and how he just wanted to write songs that sounded like Waylon's songs. Waylon smiled, and then said, "I'm sorry to hear that. If you do that, you'll always be one song behind." That's my advice to young designers. Don't be one song behind.

These interiors are my dreams. Now go and invent your own.

LOOKING BACK

by Jonah Lehrer

One of Roger Thomas's earliest memories involves the look of his hometown, Las Vegas. It was the 1950s and the city was dusty and flat; the Strip was a few casinos and nightclubs with loud, kitschy neon signs. Thomas was only a young child, but he was turned off by the loud aesthetic. "I remember being very aware of the beauty and architectural integrity found in other cities like New York, San Francisco, and Chicago," he says. He was dazzled by the skyscrapers and parks elsewhere. He wanted sidewalks and subways and historic buildings. "Even then, I never intended to stay in Las Vegas," he says.

But Thomas did end up staying in Vegas. And he didn't just stay—he transformed the look of the city. It's a metropolis now defined by its own unique aesthetic, a place full of strange and sometimes beautiful spaces that exist nowhere else on earth. They feel like the future, but Thomas's designs are not a rejection of the past—they are a remixing of history, a blend of influences that come together to create something entirely new. This is the story of how he created them.

Roger Thomas was born in 1951 in Salt Lake City. Three years later, the family moved to Las Vegas. His father, Parry Thomas, was a banker, convinced that the gaming industry represented a major business opportunity. Because legitimate banks had

refused to give casinos large construction loans, developers in Las Vegas were often forced to seek money from alternative sources. The Flamingo Hotel, for instance, had been largely financed in the 1940s with money from the New York mob. But Parry believed that Las Vegas was primed to grow, and that this city in the middle of the desolate Nevada desert would soon be a major tourist attraction.

In 1956, Parry gave the Sahara hotel a $600,000 loan; his banking colleagues thought he was crazy. But Parry had a plan—as the CEO of the Bank of Las Vegas, he was going to make sure the casinos spent his money properly. "He really was involved in every aspect of the development," Roger says. "He made sure their architecture was dramatic, featuring large marquee signs. He wanted them to hire big stars to headline their shows. He knew Las Vegas had to feel different."

The plan worked. Before long, the Strip was awash in neon lights and sprawling hotels; the clatter of slots became the soundtrack of the city. "We never lost any money on those [early] gaming loans," Parry told the journalist Jack Sheehan in his oral biography. "If they said they were going to pay back a loan on a certain day, they would pay you on that very day. They might go down the street and rob a bank to get the money, but they'd pay you."

As a child, Roger was aware of his father's importance. He knew he was the son of the man who helped build this new city. "We'd go to the big shows, and I felt special, but I was also just a kid," Roger says. "I thought everyone went to see Sinatra a few times a year. I thought every kid knew Jerry Lewis and Red Skelton and Dean Martin."

And yet, despite the success of his family, Roger struggled to fit in. "I was the weird child," he says. "What interested everyone else didn't interest me. They wanted to play sports and tennis and go waterskiing on Lake Mead. I did not." What Roger loved was drawing. He was passionate about art and design and fashion. "I'd go to the lake, but I'd bring my mother's art books," he says. "I'd read those books front to back again and again."

Roger also struggled in school. All of his siblings were straight A students, but Roger had dyslexia; his reading was labored and slow. Creativity became his consolation. "When we went to my grandparents' cabin in the Provo mountains of Utah," Roger recounts, "I would go into the woods and draw things. I learned the structure of a twig with leaves on it, to appreciate the texture of driftwood, and how rocks organize themselves in a creek." And it wasn't just drawing: Roger also taught himself to sculpt and weave and sew. By the age of eight, he was knitting his own sweaters.

After Roger had a run-in with the law at age fifteen, he was sent to boarding school—a solution he'd been advocating. The Interlochen Arts Academy had recently been featured on the cover of *Life* magazine. "My parents saw this as the solution," Roger says. "I saw this as my way out." Despite a rushed application, he was accepted. Soon after, he found himself in northern Michigan at Interlochen. "Going to Interlochen was the best thing that ever happened to me," Roger says. "For the first time, I was in a place where what I did well was valued. There was no basketball team, no football team. Instead, we had two symphony orchestras. Athletic ability and popularity had no currency at Interlochen. Only talent and creativity mattered."

Parry Thomas insisted that all his children work during the summer—they might be Vegas royalty, but they couldn't lounge by the pool. Roger's first job was at a Union Bank. His assignment was signature verification. He hated it. His next job was at Yates-Silverman, an interior design firm in Los Angeles that did work for most of the big casinos. "This job I loved right away," says Roger. "It was work that didn't feel like work. And I was able to understand everything, because it was all visual and aesthetic and I was good at it."

The following summer, Roger was given his first design project at Yates-Silverman. "Las Vegas was growing, and the family bank was adding branches," according to Roger. "They needed a new look, something to make the bank stand out." Bank design had always emphasized security, but Roger wanted to bring a new aesthetic to this branch. "I knew that the people who visited this local branch were going to be housewives cashing checks, or small businessmen getting small loans, so I thought it should feel delightful," Roger says. "It was a crazy idea, but I thought: 'What if it were fun to go to a bank?'"

The design Roger came up with had stark paper-white walls, with accent walls covered in cobalt, cherry red, and bright orange felt. He hung graphic art in plexiglass boxes, and chose furniture with thin legs, so the daylight from the glass windows at the front flooded the floor. "I took out everything that was heavy or ponderous," Roger says. "Well, except for the giant stainless-steel vault door in the center of the rear wall. That had to stay."

Roger wasn't allowed to tell his family he was working on the bank. And when Yates-Silverman presented his design, he wasn't allowed to be in the room. Nevertheless, after they presented the design, Jerry Mack—Parry's business partner for four decades—announced that it was the best thing Yates-Silverman had ever done. His only question was why they hadn't done more designs like this. It was energetic. It was attractive. It was like nothing else. "And that is how I became the bank designer," Roger says with a laugh.

In retrospect, it's easy to see the roots of Roger's style in that early design for a local Nevada bank. There is the abiding interest in joy and delight; the fusion of feeling and function—or, rather, the recognition that feeling is a central function of design; the bold (maybe even brash) use of color and light; the singular focus on the desires of his audience, those housewives looking for a dash of fun during the morning errands.

After graduating from Interlochen, Roger was accepted into the School of the Museum of Fine Arts in Boston and Tufts University. He could have graduated early based on his advanced placement from Interlochen and his craftsmanship, but he decided to stay on and pursue an extended thesis in Native American art history. "I ended up spending four and a half months traveling to Native American areas in the Southwest, looking at the textiles they were working on, and really thinking about how their style came to be," Roger says.

Degree in hand, Roger returned home to represent his family in building the first major office building in downtown Las Vegas, which had been designed by Yates-Silverman. Later, Yates-Silverman asked Roger to open a Las Vegas office. This began a twenty-five-year design partnership with Janellen Radoff.

Roger's first projects involved more bank buildings. He refined his bright brand of mid-century modernism, bringing in natural light and splashing the walls with bold colors. Before long, he started getting requests from casino owners to do their Las Vegas

houses. "Yates-Silverman hated residential design," Roger says. "They saw no profit in it. So, I got assigned to do all these houses. But then the owners liked what I did. And they would entertain other casino people. And so, they would ask me if I could also do parts of their casino interiors. I got asked to do a restaurant, I got asked to do a registration area, I got asked to do a convention facility."

At the time, Roger remained a brash young designer, steeped in modern forms. "I had absolutely no use for the history of design," he says. "I knew the history of design well enough to reject it, but I didn't know it well enough to respect it. I thought the eighteenth century was frivolous. I hadn't learned the genius of what they had done yet. If it happened before Mies van der Rohe, I wasn't interested."

But even as Roger rejected the past, he was still unconsciously influenced by it. "Looking back, the great advantage of my privileged childhood was being exposed to all these cosmopolitan experiences," he says. "I remember walking into Chartres Cathedral for the first time and seeing the neoclassical Palace of the Legion of Honor and Palazzo Colonna, and entering the vaulted space of Grand Central Station, and just being really moved by these designs and buildings as a child. Without knowing it, I was accumulating and cataloguing all these spaces that I loved and wanted to re-create that feeling, just in a different way."

In 1976, two years after opening the Las Vegas office, Roger got married for the first time, to a woman he'd known since the fourth grade. He spent the next few years settling into his success, a leading designer in a boomtown. He created the casino of the Lady Luck, which he festooned in a *Saturday Night Fever* theme. ("Thank god that's been demolished," Roger says.)

One of Roger's favorite causes was the Las Vegas Ballet Theater. At the annual dinner for the board of directors, Roger was seated next to Steve and Elaine Wynn. Wynn was the owner of the Golden Nugget, an aging downtown hotel that he'd turned into an upscale casino, featuring the fanciest guest rooms in the city. Roger had known Wynn for years, ever since

his father, Parry, had mentored Wynn in the late 1960s. "Steve was a combination of the famous Jewish financier Bernard Baruch and the showman Flo Ziegfeld," Parry told the writer Jack Sheehan. "I could see that he had talents in the gaming and hospitality industry that were enormous, far better than anybody else."

At the dinner, Steve Wynn asked Roger what he'd been up to. Roger rattled off a list of his latest projects. Steve nodded, then uttered a sentence that would change Roger's life: "I think you should work for me," Wynn said. "I'm going to build a hotel the likes of which no one's ever seen before, and I think you'd have a lot of fun doing it."

The next day, Roger was planning to accept an offer to become a named partner at Yates-Silverman. "But as soon as Steve asked me to work for him, I knew that if I said no, I would always wonder what could have been," Roger says. "Steve was so dynamic, so charismatic, so extraordinary. So, I called Charles Silverman in the morning, and I said, 'I'm very sorry. I appreciate everything you've done for me. I have learned my trade at your feet. I will never forget that, but I need to give this a try.' I went to work for Steve." Janellen Radoff would join him again a year later, and would help design the Mirage, Treasure Island, and the Bellagio. In 2000, she joined the inaugural Wynn design team.

When Roger began working with Steve Wynn on his new hotel, Las Vegas was still dominated by a design philosophy developed by Bill Friedman. Friedman distilled his research into thirteen rules, which he codified as the Friedman Casino Design Principles. Friedman, for instance, advocated the extensive use of low, blacked-out ceilings ("Principle 8: Low Ceilings beat high ceilings") and insisted that the slot machines be arranged in a confusing labyrinth ("Principle 4: The maze layout beats long, wide, straight passageways and aisles"). He was scornful of any furniture in casinos that wasn't directly related to gaming ("Principle 9: The gaming equipment as the decor beats impressive and memorable decorations") and argued that the gaming area should begin within ten feet of the entrance, if only so potential gamblers had no room to escape.

The design of these casinos, in other words, was the total absence of design—the goal of the interior was to focus all attention on the act of gaming. According to Friedman's principles, the perfect gaming space was a confusing warren of penny slots stacked to the ceiling. Nothing else was needed because the games were more than enough.

Despite the deliberate unpleasantness, Friedman's model was effective. Las Vegas gamers seemed perfectly happy to play games that were stacked against them in dim warehouses without any decor. Even Caesars Palace, which billed itself as a new kind of Vegas destination when it premiered in 1966, still featured a cave-like casino with low ceilings and no natural light. Furthermore, Friedman's textbook was dense with evidence, the pages crammed full of complicated-looking equations that linked his principles to higher player counts.

However, by the late 1970s, the first cracks started to appear in the Friedman model of casino design, as the number of visitors to Las Vegas began to plateau and then decline. The explanation for the fall was obvious: the desert city had lost

its monopoly on sin. Thanks to the growth of Atlantic City and the legalization of gaming on Native American reservations, people were now able to play the slots without traveling to Nevada.

It also didn't help that the gaming halls were such irritating places. "Every casino looked as if it had been built by two hookers and a pit boss," Roger says. "It was all red-flock wallpaper and carpets designed to hide god knows what." Although the disorienting layout of the spaces ensnared the occasional guest, it turned off casual players. "It was becoming clear to me that this way wasn't working anymore," Roger says. "You can't treat your guests like a rat in a maze."

Roger's first project with Wynn was Victoria Bay, a planned theme casino on the north end of the Strip. "It was a 'once upon a time' concept," Roger recalls. "And it was going to be the biggest hotel in the world." Wynn imagined four separate thirty-story towers containing two thousand rooms, a sprawling casino surrounded by restaurants and bars, and an ornate design that "would cause a typical person to want to walk over every inch," Wynn said.

Roger was tasked with designing the guest rooms at Victoria Bay. He settled on a radical new look. "The rooms had a taupe and white striped wall cover and a wisteria trellis that went up into a border that attached around the room to create a crown molding," Roger says. "Light colored furniture, all white finishes, and a floral carpet that was also a light background. There was a rose scheme and a lavender scheme. It was completely different from everything else in Las Vegas, but people really got it."

Roger credits Steve and Elaine Wynn with inspiring and shaping his work. "Steve always insisted, 'Think like the guest.' I changed that in my studio to 'Feel like the guest.' And Elaine always offered comments from the perspective of the most sophisticated guest and made clear that feeling let down or disappointed or bored was not an option. So, I always knew I had to deliver a design that really made our guests feel elevated."

Unfortunately, Victoria Bay was never built, a victim of higher interest rates and the recession of 1980–81. (The guest rooms Roger designed became the new guest rooms at the Golden Nugget instead.) But Wynn continued to pursue his vision of a Vegas mega resort. After selling his Atlantic City property in a bidding war between Bally's and Donald Trump, Wynn had the financing to begin working on the Mirage, a sprawling 3,044-room hotel with a tropical theme. "It was inspired by Hawaii and the Caribbean and the islands," Roger says. "There was going to be an atrium in the middle of the hotel with giant palm trees, and a volcano in the front

yard and Siegfried and Roy making tigers disappear in the showroom. But it was also going to be elegant and refined, the first hotel developed in Las Vegas where the restaurants were going to be a major contributor to the bottom line. No longer was the food going to be a loss leader. We wanted to create restaurants and bars and spaces that were so good and so beautiful that people would come just for them."

Consider the ice cream parlor, a small space in the back of the Mirage. "I went to town with this parlor," Roger says. "I lacquered the space with tropical, crazy colors: turquoise, fuchsia, mango, yellow, lime. I believed that if you elevate the experience of guests, they're going to love it. They might not get it, they might not even appreciate it, but all those little details add up. They remember the surprise and return for more."

The success of the Mirage inspired a frenzy of imitation, as developers raced to construct their own themed mega resorts. Before long, the Strip featured a giant pyramid clad in dark bronze glass (The Luxor), a fake New York skyline and Statue of Liberty (New York, New York), and a 541-foot-tall model of the Eiffel Tower (Paris Las Vegas). Although these hotels were all successful—the growth of Vegas seemed insatiable, with the number of tourists tripling between 1980 and 2000—Roger came to believe that this design strategy was a dead end, turning the Strip into a cheap caricature of a real city.

"It's really such a lazy approach," he says. "These companies build gigantic towers that have no sense of scale, no sense

of intimacy, no sense of flow, and then they try to hide all the flaws behind a stucco copy of some famous structure." Roger refers to such designs as "replitecture," dismissing them as shoddy imitations of the real thing.

After the incredible success of the Mirage, Roger's design talents were in high demand. Wynn put him in charge of the entire interior of Treasure Island, a companion hotel to the Mirage, then asked him to develop new ideas for the forthcoming Bellagio, which Steve and Elaine Wynn insisted would be "the most extraordinary hotel on planet Earth." After a divorce, Roger had married Andrea Thomas, a former Yates-Silverman colleague, and they had a child, Drew. Eventually, the professional pressure got to Roger. "By then I had found the relief of the cocktail," he says. "The work itself wasn't the problem—it was itself a high, and both fueled and excused my drinking. Travel was also an opportunity to indulge." Five months into the Bellagio design, Roger had a near-death experience after mixing alcohol and Valium. "I ended

up in rehab after that episode," Roger says. "That was over twenty-five years ago. And when I came out of rehab on my birthday, I was reborn, I was just ready to change my life. I had this unstoppable energy. My imagination was running rampant. And that's how the worst thing that ever happened to me became the best thing that ever happened to me."

Sobriety transformed Roger's work. He was now able to fully focus on his craft, creating a signature look that existed nowhere else in the industry. It was an audacity he'd learned in part from Andy Warhol, whom he'd gotten to know while spending time in New York City. "Andy had a remarkable influence on me," Roger says. "On the one hand, he was the most timid, afraid kind of guy. But he had this extraordinary confidence in his art, in what he created. I related to that, because I was basically afraid of everybody and everything, but I learned from him that the fear doesn't have to limit you. If you trust your instincts, and you do it with total conviction, then the work will resonate. So that's what I increasingly tried to do in my designs."

Roger's inspiration for the Bellagio came from numerous trips to northern Italy and the South of France. He became an inveterate sketcher; his black Hermès notebook was always in hand. Whenever he noticed a form that caught his eye—and it didn't matter if it was a picture frame at the Louvre or a crumbling stone wall on a highway outside Florence—he was inspired by the form. But he didn't begin drawing yet—Roger only got out his notebook after he left the thing behind. "The passage of a few hours can be very revealing," he says. "Memory is a filter."

While touring Europe, Roger also had the chance to develop relationships with leading artisans. He worked with Venetian chandelier fabricators, who were able to create the ornate designs in his sketchbook. He met the Rubelli family, renowned for their fabrics, and worked closely with them on creating textiles that could be used at the scale needed for a Las Vegas resort. "They understood that I couldn't use their silk fabrics that cost $250 a yard," he says. "But we put our heads together and created a version for $39 a yard that looked like the original and was very durable. You can get what you want combined with what you need when you purchase by the kilometer."

Elaine Wynn also became an essential collaborator. "If I had a new idea, I'd usually go to Elaine first to get her opinion—I just had to promise to not tell Steve," Roger says with a wry smile. Roger would often fall in love with a particular product, charmed by its history or narrative. But Elaine was gifted at seeing the big picture, how the product would fit into the overall guest experience. "I'd show her some fabric I discovered in Europe, and she'd admire it, but then point out that it might not be right for the overall space," Roger says. "She always pushed me to make the designs more layered, more emotional, more dramatic."

Elaine saw her role primarily as an editor for Roger:

> The initial designs he showed me were usually home runs. I might ask for a little more or a little less, or maybe a different color or that something be a little more tailored for female guests, but he rarely needed much feedback. I'd known Roger for so long—ever since he was a child—that it was easy to lose sight of the fact that he was also a genius. But sometimes I'd see one of his spaces, and it would be full of these elements that taken separately you'd never see working together, but Roger made it work. A lot of people try to be eclectic and don't succeed. Roger succeeds. He knows how to take it right to the edge but no further.

Las Vegas is a city built on ephemeral designs: even the biggest hotels are torn down on a regular basis in pursuit of the latest trends, whether it's the "replitecture" of the Venetian or the corporate modernism of City Center. But as Roger traveled around Europe, he became increasingly fascinated with the enduring forms of classic design. "I'd look at these designs that were five-hundred-years-old but no one ever got tired of," he says. "Why not? It's not because they've got Ionic columns, or some other historic element. It's because they got the essence of form right: perfection of proportion and scale. If you understand the essences of classical design, you can design everything from a cocktail table to a forty-story building. It doesn't matter what the thing is because it's about how the form relates to the human mind, the human eye. That's why it's classic. That's why it lasts."

The Bellagio became an audacious experiment. It's as if Roger was deliberately violating every one of Bill Friedman's principles for casino design, rejecting those time-tested rules of Las Vegas architecture. The first principle of "Designing Casinos", for instance, criticized the "open barn" plan, which Friedman defined as any space with an expansive layout and high ceilings. But Roger's design for the Bellagio casino called for soaring ceilings cloaked in billowing silk and clear sight

lines for easy navigation. The second principle in Friedman's textbook called for "gambling equipment immediately inside casino entrances," placing those slot machines with the best odds by the front door. Roger and the Wynns, however, imagined an elegant and expansive lobby. Instead of filling the space with loud penny slots, Roger spent several million dollars on a massive Dale Chihuly glass sculpture and insisted on huge bouquets of real flowers. Although traditional casinos barred clocks and glimpses of the sun—Friedman wanted gamers to lose track of the time—Roger installed antique clocks and, at Wynn's insistence, massive skylights.

The Bellagio was an incredible success, generating the largest profits for a single property in Las Vegas history. (And this income wasn't a by-product of scale, as the Bellagio was less than half the size of the 6,852-room MGM Grand.) What's more, it was the first Las Vegas resort in which non-gaming revenue surpassed gaming revenue. Roger's design proved to be extremely influential, not only for casinos but also for the wider hospitality industry. "Las Vegas is a very liberating place to be a designer," Roger says. "Nobody is hung up on authenticity. They just want to know if the room works."

In 2000, Wynn sold the Mirage and the Bellagio to MGM Resorts. But Wynn wasn't ready to retire. Before long, the Wynns and Roger were at work on their next luxurious resort, which would be even grander and more beautiful. "Steve called the Bellagio our trial hotel, our learning curve," Roger says. "And he used to say we made a lot of mistakes at Bellagio. But we're going to correct every one of them. And we did."

Wynn decided that this new hotel would not reference a particular region, like the Mirage or the Bellagio. Rather, it would seek to evoke the feel of luxury itself, an opulence freed from the limitations of time and place. Wynn gave Roger the following mandate: "I want it to be something no one has ever seen before. Totally unique." Roger realized that, in order to fulfill Wynn's wish, he would have to invent a new design language, starting with an alphabet of shapes, forms, colors, and details.

As usual, Roger began with his notebooks, searching for those designs that he'd never been able to implement anywhere else. He brought in a daybed inspired by the shape of an Italian greyhound's hind leg and filled the lobby with giant pendant lights made of moving parasols, or colorful umbrellas. "I've always been enchanted by parasols," he says. "I love their shape, their whimsy, the way light filters through them." Of course, his sketches proved difficult to implement, which is why Roger spent three and half years commuting several times a week to a remote factory in the desert.

But sometimes the notebooks weren't enough: Roger wanted his custom furniture to be interspersed with authentic artifacts, giving the resort a sense of worldliness unheard of in Vegas. (He'd become convinced that real things were the best critique of "replitecture.") In Bartolotta Ristorante di Mare, an Italian seafood restaurant on the Wynn Lake, Roger decided to decorate the grand staircase with three six-foot-tall olive jars that predated the Second World War. Unfortunately, it proved surprisingly hard to find additional olive jars, which meant that his team was forced to spend two years scouring antiques stores in Italy, Greece, London, and Los Angeles. In a sly homage to Vegas history, the crystals dangling from the terra-cotta jugs were scavenged from the Desert Inn, the old Howard Hughes property that was demolished to make room for the Wynn. "I like to think that Howard's ghost is still hanging around here," Roger says.

Steve and Elaine Wynn gave Roger tremendous freedom to invent these interiors. "Not only did they allow me extraordinary latitude and unheard-of budgets, but they always challenged me to achieve more than I thought myself capable," Roger says. The Wynns were the perfect patrons for a designer looking to reinvent the look of the Las Vegas hotel.

When it came to the design of the casino, however, nothing was left to chance. Wynn commissioned a full-scale model of the main gaming space in a warehouse at a cost of nearly $3 million. (The final bill for the 5.2-million-square-foot hotel would approach $2.8 billion, or nearly $750,000 per guest room.) This allowed Roger and Wynn to test and refine every single design element in the gaming area, from the Jacques Garcia carpet to the lumbar support in the blackjack chairs to the chandeliers over the card tables, which make the vast casino feel like a collection of intimate dining areas. "No one had ever put chandeliers over gaming before," Roger says. "And that's because the fixture gets in the way of the security cameras." It took eighteen months of patient engineering, but Roger found a way to get a camera into the chandelier itself.

This same obsessive study even went into the scent of the hotel. Although most casinos rely on musky scents to mask the odor of cigarette smoke, Wynn insisted on a light, fresh scent called "Asian Rain." "The ultimate goal was drama," Roger says. "It's an interior design that expresses drama, romance, mystery, and joy. The curves, the color, the dark brown against the white, the scent . . . The goal was to create spaces that make you feel like your best self, that incorporate history with my influences but combine them in ways that feel new and risky and different. If you've seen it before, then it's not going to be very interesting, is it?"

But it wasn't enough to be beautiful or interesting. As Elaine Wynn points out, Roger's spaces also had to perform. "You have to remember that our hotels are open twenty-four hours a day, seven days a week. Even Disneyland closes for cleanup and repairs—but we never close. So, Roger's designs have to be elegant and extremely durable. If you find a beautiful fabric, it can't just be beautiful. It also has to endure hundreds of people sitting on it every day."

The late art critic Dave Hickey appreciated Las Vegas: he considered the Strip to be one of the great urban boulevards in the world, a spectacle of public art and design. Hickey credited Roger with creating much of that spectacle and ensuring that it was more than just ersatz imitations. "Roger elevated everything in this city," Hickey said. "He's got great taste, but he also knows everything. He knows the dude in Venice who blows the glass and can rattle off the sixteenth-century Italian tapestry maker that inspired the carpet in the men's bathroom. His stuff has layers, but you don't need to get the layers to appreciate it."

At the heart of Hickey's writing is a belief in the democratization of beauty, a conviction that everyone should have access to immersive aesthetic experiences. That's one of the things he loved about Roger's work: it gave the public access to some of the most sumptuous and luxurious spaces in the world. They might not get the layers of historical references, but they could still feel them. "These are special spaces, and they are open to the street," Hickey says. "How many buildings can you walk into on the Champs-Élysées?"

Since creating the Wynn, Roger has gone on to incorporate the same dramatic themes at the Encore, Wynn Macau, Wynn Palace Cotai, and Encore Boston Harbor. He's been awarded countless design honors, including being named five times to the AD100 and to the *Interior Design* Hall of Fame. In 2020, Roger became an adviser to Wynn Resorts, giving up the position of executive vice president he'd held for nearly two decades. "The enduring value of the Wynn brand is Roger Thomas design," Elaine says. "That is what our guests ultimately experience—his designs. His genius."

Roger hasn't stopped creating beautiful things. Our most recent interview took place at the Quintus showroom in the Pacific Design Center, Los Angeles. (Roger is a partner at Quintus.) In between telling stories about old Las Vegas resorts, he'd offer direction to the staff on lighting angles and rug placement. "Excuse me for a moment," he'd say mid-sentence, and then wander over to adjust an accessory. His eyes never stopped moving, assessing, searching for ways to improve the room.

That said, Roger does seem to be enjoying a break from the scale and pressure of hotel design. He is now married to Arthur Libera, a licensing agent for artists and designers, and they divide their time between Venice and the West Coast. In many respects, Roger's latest projects mark a return to his early roots in craftsmanship. For instance, he recently completed a stunning micromosaic jewelry collection, a form of decorative arts that's so labor intensive it all but disappeared during the twentieth century, for SICIS. "I was a goldsmithing major at Interlochen, and I've always loved working with metal and setting jewels in metal," Roger says. He still gets visibly excited by a well-crafted piece of art or furniture, his voice vibrating when he describes the emotional power of a Titian altarpiece, or the elegant curves of an eighteenth-century French chair.

"I still try to draw every inspiration that comes my way," Roger says. "I don't draw because I need to—I just draw what I feel is beautiful. And then later, when I need to create something new, I can go back to my books. But that's where it begins. If you're not looking out for beauty, then what are you looking for?"

DRAMA

When a person walks
into a dramatic room,
there's a signature tell:

you can hear their inhalation, like a little gasp. That's the sound of drama, an immersive experience that compels people to keep looking. It's design at its most cinematic.

How does one create drama with design? For me, it begins with contrast, creating juxtapositions that are unexpected and interesting. Take the Wynn. I started with a high-contrast color palette: chocolate brown and white. That was a unique combination that I'd never seen before in a hotel.

But the colors are just the start. I also create contrast with textures, situating very smooth surfaces like a pleated silk fabric next to very textured ones.

And then there's the scale of things. I might contrast a live bouquet of flowers with a large floral mural. Grand interiors with vaulted ceilings are next to intimate spaces—I learned that from Frank Lloyd Wright—which creates a sense of movement between expansion and compression.

Lighting is also essential for drama. As I always say, "Good interiors with bad lighting are bad interiors." That's why I've always been obsessive about the quality of lighting in our interiors, whether it's the tropical mansard huts at the Mirage or the moving parasol lights at the Wynn.

One last point about drama: more isn't always better. Too much drama can be overbearing, a relentless source of tension that makes you want to leave. The drama makes you pay attention, but it still has to be alluring and sensual.

You want that gasp of amazement, but you also want to create a space that's a pleasure to be in.

This was my original design for the Wynn Macau Wing Lei Restaurant's Private Dining Room. I created drama with the unexpected scale of the carpet design and the huge chandelier, the entire concept a response to Steve's demand to avoid the design clichés of the typical Chinese restaurant (page 22). Dragons are ubiquitous in Chinese cuisine, but at the Wynn Macau Wing Lei Restaurant we reinvigorated the cliché with a twenty-seven-foot-long crystal dragon lit from within. I had ninety days to create this beautiful monster, whose head is a single piece of cast glass that weighs 650 pounds (previous spread). The Wynn Macau Wing Lei Restaurant is the most visited restaurant at the hotel, and after many years we wanted to reestablish guest interest, which we did with drama, creating dramatic focal points at every turn as you enter the restaurant (opposite, top and bottom). Comfortable seating areas in the reception area at the Wynn Macau Wing Lei Restaurant allow guests to enjoy an exceptional selection of teas while they wait (below). We retained the signature crystal dragon at the Wynn Macau Wing Lei Restaurant, but completely redesigned the room, adding giant lampshades with inner brass chandeliers, festooned with lacquer orange tassels. The dining chairs are my own design, inspired by classic Ming dynasty examples I saw in Hong Kong. The embroidery on the backs of the chairs matches the embroidery on the tablecloths and napkins (following spread).

To honor China, we wanted to reinvent chinoiserie for the twenty-first century. The VIP Private Reception room at the Wynn Cotai Palace is a cushiony vault of shimmering gold and white with dramatic accents of jade green and a collection of heroically scaled cloisonné vases. The reception desk front is rare emerald green travertine inlaid with brass and white mother-of-pearl (below). Space is the ultimate luxury in China. We emphasized the dramatic double-height ceiling in this private villa at the Wynn Cotai Palace with fully embroidered satin tiebacks and tassel holdbacks that are over six feet long. The beaded central chandelier, pavéed with hundreds of cut crystal beads, is seven feet in diameter (opposite, top). This exceptional screen, a masterpiece of eighteenth-century Chinese lacquer, was returned to China from a British collection. At the Wynn Cotai Palace, it sits atop an eighteen-foot-wide custom credenza with antique coromandel screen inlays. The large Venetian glass chandeliers were designed to honor the lotus flower in Chinese culture (opposite, bottom).

Each of these three cast-bronze vases is over fifteen feet tall. These giant versions of classic Chinese ceramics were created as the focal point to an enfilade of swimming pools viewed from the entry lobby at the Wynn Macau. Drama at a distance requires heroic scale (previous spread). Looking from the giant vases back to the entry lobby at the Wynn Macau, a pair of seven-foot-tall cloisonné camels float on the surface of the upper pool. This dramatic feature was added one week before opening. When Steve Wynn felt that something was missing from the view from the entry lobby, I realized that I needed a foreground element. This was my solution, which I sourced from a secret Hong Kong vendor. The camels were placed in the dark of night to surprise Steve at sunrise the next morning (left and above).

One entire wall of Café Encore at the Encore Macau is a hand-painted canvas, inspired by Venetian Renaissance master Paolo Veronese's largest paintings, both of which were banquet scenes. My dear friends Charley Brown and Mark Evans integrated the two compositions to create this joyous image of dining at its most raucous. American ceramic artist Joan Bankemper created the foreground object, which is a sculptural collage composed of both Chinese and American ceramics (previous spread). This entire room—the Encore Macau Bar Cristal—was designed around the early eighteenth-century Empire chandelier at its center, which I'd found in Brussels two years earlier. Cut crystal and glass were used at the center of all four walls; one surface was composed of a hundred tiny Venetian mirrors and fronted by faceted glass shelves with cut crystal stemware and glasses. The collective shimmer was made even more dramatic by the polished mahogany and French blue color scheme of the entire room (opposite and below).

The design of the guest reception area at the Encore Las Vegas Resort began when Elaine Wynn and I found a pair of Garouste and Bonetti torchères at Art Basel Miami Beach, which I placed behind the onyx registration desk, flanked by giant red lacquered flowers and jeweled dragonflies on an overscale woven abaca texture custom-dyed to match—a material made for floors that we used on the wall. Imaginary butterfly designs flutter across the carpet (previous spread). Unexpected drama is created in the lobby of the Wynn Encore Macau by the giant aquarium with live jellyfish. An entire marine department concealed behind the front desk supports this magic. The chandelier in the center contains no lights—it is illuminated entirely from the edges of the soffit (pages 20–21, above, and opposite). Slot machines with pay-outs up to $25,000 enjoy a garden room atmosphere, in what was originally a nightclub space at the Wynn Las Vegas. The golden lotus fountain and seating and lounge area with a garden surround are the last things guests expect to find when playing slots (following spread).

The redesign of Mizumi, a restaurant at the Wynn Las Vegas, centered on opening an entire exterior wall to a view of a seventy-five-foot-tall waterfall and koi pond in the private garden beyond. This view is framed by two enormous golden koi on red lacquered pedestals. The lacquered walls feature collections of exquisite obi, the sash used for formal kimonos. The design of one of these obi inspired the carpeting, and a red Japanese crest is embroidered on the back of each leather chair (below and opposite).

I inherited this room at the Wynn Las Vegas, which featured several walls of natural stacked limestone. I began by sealing the limestone behind the bar and leafing it with real gold as a background for a collection of Noh theater masks—drama direct from the Japanese stage. Lintels and beams were lacquered red to dramatically contrast with the gilded and natural stone and to honor a favorite Japanese material (opposite and below).

Steve Wynn has a genius for surprise and drama, particularly in the creation of the guest experience. One of the extraordinary advantages of the architecture and layout for this premier resort in Las Vegas was the creation of five private lagoons centered on dining and entertainment. We surrounded the private pond of Bartolotta Ristorante di Mare, an elevated Italian dining experience, with private cabanas, some featuring crystal chandeliers. To solve the problem of lighting the pool yet not having a light source in the eyes of any of the guests seated nearby, I decided not to light the pool, but to install a grid of twenty-four-inch-diameter polished steel balls, which reflect the light of the surrounding areas (previous spread). These curved escalators transport guests to the restaurant and bar level at the Wynn Encore Boston Harbor. They oppose each other, making for a delightfully voyeuristic experience, as guests move up and down in opposite directions. Viola Frey's *Giant Amphora* centers the space with its unexpected scale. Lattice-covered columns have been positioned to maximize the illusion of the length of the escalators and the drama of their opposing curves. Two of the columns are structural and two were added to increase the spectacle of this very cinematic stage set (left). Guests of the exclusive Tower Suites at the Wynn Las Vegas enter the resort through this extraordinary greenhouse atrium. A view through the glass canopy reveals the entire fifty-two-story tower rising above. To further enhance the drama, the chandelier in the center of the room, created in the mountains above Marrakech, is a giant version of a familiar lantern. Koi play in the dark green ponds that edge the railings of the mosaic paths (below).

This corridor in the spa at the Wynn Las Vegas is always whisper quiet, the floor carpeted in thick wool, and the dark sapphire walls with white plum blossoms have deep articulations to quiet any noise. Soft music emerges from an unknown source. I accomplished this great drama with the interior-lit onyx columns, topped with large Murano glass vases (below). The drama of this entry to the spa at the Wynn Macau comes from the textured walls framing hand-painted silk koi swimming among lotuses. The scene is illuminated at the floor by soft lanterns, and from the ceiling by kinetic light projections that send shimmering motions across the painted ponds (right). At the Wynn Encore Boston Harbor casino bar and grand stair, the dramatic intimacy is brought to the bar in this two-story space by the staircase, with the torchères that flank the risers and the huge, red Venetian chandeliers overhead. The ninety-five chandeliers in this casino were originally installed in a sister property in Las Vegas and represented the largest order of Rubino red glass in the history of Murano. They were carefully dismantled and brought East to grace the casino bar and grand stair at the Wynn Encore Boston Harbor. The entire design was conceived to feature these unique light sculptures, each with the form of a twirling skirt (following spread).

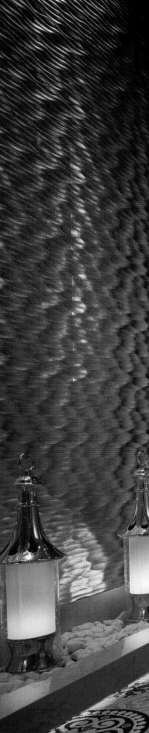

Featuring extraordinary Mandarin cuisine, the Wing Lei Restaurant is the most important restaurant in the Wynn Cotai Palace. A dozen seven-foot-tall porcelain vases flank the entry and rise from recessed collars of fuchsia and orange flowers; the vases feature arrangements of the same flowers. In reinventing chinoiserie for the twenty-first century, I designed a series of lanterns, inspired by those I saw in Asia. These are made of solid brass, and the light is diffused by white linen. Jade green tassels add an element of surprise and match the embroidery on the backs of the chairs and the crystal water glasses on the table (above). This gaming area at the Wynn Palace Cotai offers our guests private rooms for high-stakes games, a luxe space to escape the hustle and bustle of the casino. This corridor, with its faceted gold mirror, barrel-vaulted ceiling, and lotus-inspired Murano chandeliers leads to two such spaces. Polished white lacquer pilasters trimmed in brass frets, lacquered sycamore-fronted consoles, and Murano glass lamps flank doors opening to the quiet private salons (right). The City of Paris department store in San Francisco inspired the windows in this oval dining room overlooking the pool at the Wynn Las Vegas. I had purchased the originals for use at the Bellagio and couldn't get them out of my head. For the color, I found a piece of broken lattice in the gardens of the Petite Trianon at Versailles and brought it back to have the color reproduced for this garden room. The central chandelier is another of my creations constructed on the island of Murano (following spread).

ROMANCE

One of the best spaces I've ever done is also the most romantic.

It's a two-story restaurant in the Wynn. Elaine Wynn had remembered being in Sun Valley and how every woman looked forward to dressing because you'd descend a staircase into the lodge dining area. I wanted to do something similar at our restaurant, so there's a very grand curved staircase and when a woman walks down everyone looks up. The room stops. It's quite a moment.

But it's also a moment that depends on getting a million little details exactly right; romance is fragile. That's why we spent months researching and testing the right light temperature before settling on 2700 kelvins. It's why we always tried to put light at the sides of the face, and not above. Side light is more flattering. And we want you to look good. One thing I learned early on is that I feel better in a room when the people around me look better.

If you want romance in a room, then you need flowers. I insisted on lavish bouquets throughout the entire hotel—when the Wynn opened, we had forty-seven florists on staff. And it's not just flowers—Steve and Elaine and I thought garden views were very romantic, so we tried to orient as many rooms as possible to the gardens. The Wynn had five lagoons because lagoons are romantic—you have the shimmer off the water—so we create spaces where that shimmer is brought inside.

There's something about the handmade that is romantic. You can feel the craft, it's very evocative. I learned that from the Bellagio—we had these extraordinary handmade chandeliers from Murano. We even developed fully glass beaded chandeliers, so the light sparkled and left some tracery on the walls. That's the sort of romantic effect that comes from the handmade.

Certain forms also have a romantic quality. When we were designing the Wynn, we decided to base the recurring motifs on the female form. From the molding profiles to the tower itself—there's a curvilinear shape woven into all the spaces.

More than anything else, romance is a mood. It's a spell created by the interplay of the light and the flowers and the sound of the fountain and the glittering chandelier and the music.

We have five senses. You have to seduce them all.

My first successful nightclub, Blush, at the Wynn Las Vegas, included this marvelous garden space. We separated the outdoor hideaway from the rest of the resort with a leafy green hedge and white lattice twinkling with white lights. Mirrors are romantic because you can check out the action in the room without staring at someone. This reflection shows a ceiling composed of more than five hundred lampshade light fixtures with a nearly infinite number of LightJockey-controlled lighting patterns that hover above the dance floor and can be synchronized to the music. I had ninety days to transform the space; using stock lampshades stacked together for this animated ceiling was a lifesaver (page 62). The Alex Restaurant at the Wynn Las Vegas is my favorite of all the spaces I've created. It is both romantic and dramatic. The staircase entrance provides an extraordinary cinematic moment, when beautiful women glide down into the room. Everything in the room is bespoke, from the chandeliers to the chairs, and even includes the handmade carpeting and walls of mahogany intarsia (previous spread). The walls of the private dining room are draped with copper-colored silk taffeta with appliqués of handmade silk rose clusters. The lighting, inspired by André Arbus, is handmade Murano glass; the beaded trim for the silk shades is from Pottery Barn. Designed to be comfortable, the chairs were inspired by the hind leg of Steve Wynn's dog, Paolo. Each chair back top is distinguished with a small silk frog (above). At the top of the staircase is a beautiful bar area with mahogany walls and lavishly detailed upholstered seating. I designed the daybed to match the hind legs of my Italian greyhound, Bianca (opposite).

At the Encore Las Vegas Sinatra Restaurant and Bar, the tall Sicilian obelisks flanking the bar and the crystal ship chandelier came from the Paris flea market. They originally graced a 1920s Italian restaurant in the French capital and were just being delivered to the dealer's stall. When I first encountered them, I passed—I had nothing like them on my shopping list. But then I realized I could create a space around them. Nothing is as romantic as candlelight filtered through cut crystal. My best purchase ever (opposite, top). The Sinatra Restaurant at the Las Vegas Encore was so successful that Steve asked me to create a version in Boston. I used the same design vocabulary, right down to the small, shaded candles at the center of every table. Each guest is illuminated by the soft glow of candlelight. I found a remarkable light pendant in alabaster and statuary bronze by Parisian virtuoso Hervé van der Straeten to take the place of honor (opposite, bottom). The most romantic sound is the music of Frank Sinatra, whose family gave me access to their collected photos to select the perfect images for the Sinatra Restaurant at the Encore Boston Harbor. The floor-to-ceiling windows overlook the Mystic River and the Boston skyline. Everything is special: raw sandblasted oak walls, custom lettuce-colored wall upholstery, and plush wool carpeting to keep the acoustics suitable for conversation (below). Creating outdoor spaces for every restaurant and entertainment venue was one of Steve's genius moves. This famed nightclub—XS, at the Encore Las Vegas—featured a large, tiled pool. By day it was a European pool for adults only and at night it became the perfect place to be seen (following spread).

Romance is important in a bedroom. We emphasized the curved silhouette of the female form in selections of furniture and accessories, and selected colors that flatter every complexion for the tower suites at the Wynn Las Vegas: we built a model of this room and invited many guests, so that we could see how they looked in it. The Matisse is a reproduction of a drawing in Steve's collection that was printed in a limited edition by permission of the artist's estate (opposite, top). Personal romance can be increased by notions of both privacy and sharing. Many of the suites, and all villas, at the Wynn Macau feature separate his and hers bathrooms. This beautiful bathroom, with a view of the South China Sea, is only for her, unless she invites someone to share the large, jetted bathtub (opposite, bottom). The rooftop garden villas at the Wynn Palace Cotai had two or three matching master bedrooms, each extravagant. The view through the floor-to-ceiling window is to a private swimming pool that's more than a hundred feet long and framed by an enfilade of urns and olive trees. The brass framed screen behind the bed is covered in hand-embroidered Chinese silk (above).

At the Wynn Las Vegas, there are only six lavish villa suites with this golf course view. As you can imagine they are in high demand. You would never know from the lush and lavish landscaping that this photograph was taken about three months after planting. It took some doing but we got safety code approval for this whimsical custom handrail (previous spread). You should feel pampered in bathrooms, especially at the Wynn Palace Cotai. The number of precious materials used in these small spaces can be extraordinary. Rare Grecian marble, hand-blown glass, Italian mosaics, gilded chrysanthemums floating on mirrors, four golden amphora of my own design—all combine to make one feel one's best (above). In the private dining corridor at the Wynn Palace Cotai, this dramatically scaled vase, covered in seashells, is the work of artist Thomas Boog, a Parisian master of the art of *coquillage*. This now lost art was used in many romantic spaces of the eighteenth century, decorating walls, ceilings, and grotto hideaways—places to be alone, surrounded by the mysteries of the sea and the sound of splashing water (opposite). Maximizing the Encore Boston Harbor's tower over the Mystic River, we customized pop-up televisions for uninterrupted bedside cityscape enjoyment (following spread).

Once upon a time is always romantic. I love to create special vignettes like this one with a nineteenth-century bronze sculpture, reflected in an early twentieth-century Venetian mirror, against a hand-embroidered wall cover. The white lacquer and gold-leaf console was designed just for this space in the Encore Boston Harbor reception area (above). A pair of these exquisite nineteenth-century French terra-cotta figures of spring and summer goddesses traveled from hotel to hotel, from Las Vegas to China to Boston. Of all the locations they have graced, they never looked more at home, or more perfectly romantic, than among the flower beds of the garden lobby in the Encore Boston Harbor, flanking the curved escalators (right). Drama can be very simple. At Encore Boston Harbor's Garden Bar, the contrast of the apple-green upholstery and the dark framed seating creates a dramatic impact that doesn't lessen the softness of this elegant hideaway's atmosphere. The garden green recaps the lush atrium planting on the overlook edge of the bar. Creamy coloring and mirrors embellish the surrounding walls. This is a favorite meeting spot; guests can observe each other with discretion in the mirrors (following spread).

SURPRISE

One of the ways I achieve surprise in a design is to ask:

What should we absolutely not do in this room? The answer to that question leads to surprise. It helps you think about the subtle expectations we have for certain spaces.

When we were designing the Chinese restaurant at the Wynn Macau, the initial design was red, gold, and burgundy. Steve walked in when it was being put together and said, "You have to do something. It looks exactly like a Chinese restaurant." I was in Las Vegas, but immediately got to work incorporating surprise.

I changed the colors to periwinkle, lime green, and orange. Those are the colors of a tropical bar, not a Chinese restaurant. We installed furniture that felt suited for a contemporary French dining room. Instead of a carved wooden dragon, which was the expected choice, I designed an enormous 27-foot-long Chinese dragon illuminated sculpture.

But how to build it? I finally found a craftsman who created large cruise ship replicas for travel agents. It took countless iterations, but we eventually made a beautiful dragon covered in cut crystals. This was yet another reminder that surprise is hard work; inventing crystal dragons is never easy.

It's always easier to conform to cliches and expectations. It's also less satisfying.

The best surprises have layers to them. For instance, at the Wynn, we had a walkway by the fishpond and gardens. We suspended lantern lights in the trees. At night, the light of the lanterns is reflected in the water as you walk along the path. It's a continually unfolding sense of discovery.

Surprise should also reward attention. It's why I created a chandelier made of glittering goldfish that look like they're swimming. It's why, when you walk to the Tower suites at the Wynn Las Vegas, we installed a ceiling made of glass. If you look up, you see the tower above you. The sheer scale is a surprise.

The design of surprise requires a willingness to surprise yourself, too. When we were working on the Encore, I was shopping at the Paris flea market with my team. I had my list. But then I saw these two crystal beaded ten-foot tall obelisks and ship chandelier. Needless to say, these were not on my list. So I walked away. I immediately walked back. I had no idea where they'd go. But I knew that I needed them and bought them on the spot.

What did I do with them? Those became the esssence of surprise for the Sinatra Restaurant and Bar at the Encore.

The crystal dragon in Macau quickly became an icon. We decided to use it as the centerpiece of a new restaurant with Asian cuisine in Las Vegas, Wazuzu at the Encore. This is the most popular dining table in the room as the dragon curves above the table, illuminating everyone in the soft glow of its scales. It's a truly unique and unexpected experience—and a real opportunity for a fantastic selfie (page 84). While the first decoration of the Bartolotta Ristorante di Mare, a bastion of Italian cuisine in Las Vegas, featured giant antique terra-cotta olive oil jars, the second iteration focused on seafood, imported daily from the Adriatic. The Monterey Bay Aquarium inspired the school of golden fish. It connects the upper-level bar and dining area and the lower-level dining room, which is accessed by a sweeping staircase. Large koi swim in the pool at the center of the dining room, contributing to a truly unique culinary experience (previous spread). I discovered this antique galleon-shaped chandelier, of handmade glass, beads, and wire, at the Paris flea market. It delights and surprises with its very presence (above). Chandeliers inspired by the ropes that are ubiquitous to sailing vessels, especially galleons, center the room. I had the hemp cords dyed olive green and strung with cast-resin spheres in the same color, to surround glass cylinders hand-painted with a tree-green linen texture. On the ceiling, stucco carved ropes in what I called drunken loops repeat the motif (right).

Steve Wynn and Tom Fazio completely redesigned the old Desert Inn golf course to become the incomparable Wynn Golf Course and Country Club. Club restaurant guests enjoy this extraordinary view of the huge waterfall next to the 18th hole. Golf carts headed for the clubhouse disappear behind the cascade (below). This glowing dining terrace of the Botero Restaurant at the Wynn Encore Las Vegas is surrounded by formal French parterre gardens—an unexpected pavilion at the very center of the hotel (opposite, top). This eighteen-foot-tall centerpiece of a flight of imaginary butterflies is constructed of a stainless-steel armature covered with colorful Italian glass mosaics created in Ravenna and graces the porte cochere of the Wynn Encore Las Vegas. Butterflies were used as a design motif throughout the entire resort. They epitomize beauty, nobility, and abundance across the world. The designs were not taken from nature, but from my imagination—fanciful exercises in my sketchbook (opposite, bottom).

When we opened the Hotel Bellagio, we realized that we could have created better views of the magnificent fountains for our guests as they were dining. We corrected that mistake by positioning the Teatro Ristorante above the porte cochere adjacent to the enormous fountain display in the front of the Wynn Macau. Guests are astounded by sudden bursts of aquatic choreography synchronized with the music in the room while enjoying exceptional Italian cuisine in the heart of this South Asian metropolis. A lavish mountain of flowers centers the six-foot-diameter black lacquer pedestal at the entry, separating arrival, relaxation, and dining (previous spread). At the Wynn Macau, guests enter a shimmer of gold and white to encounter a matched pair of chinoiserie aquarium cabinets filled with rare goldfish, as well as a wall of live, colorful fragrant flowers dancing on a lattice pattern carved mirror behind the gilded-glass registration desk. There's also a floral-laden center table, floating on a hand-set Italian-glass mosaic floor of ancient cloud designs. The flowers in both displays change with the seasons (above and right).

I inherited a restaurant—Mizumi at the Wynn Macau—of beautiful design to reimagine. Natural blond-ash walls were lacquered red or covered in a wall covering I developed for Maya Romanoff made of cinnabar-colored vinyl combed with a tool made by a violin maker. The exquisite woven obi mounted on the focal wall were acquired from a favorite dealer in Paris. They literally traveled around the world to this room in southeast China. The drapery, woven on an Italian loom in a shimmer of gold, frames the garden view (left). In Mizumi at the Wynn Macau, we gold-leafed the natural stone walls and lacquered the framing walls in brilliant red. The enameled Ferrari-yellow metal origami dog sculpture by American artist Gerardo Hacer came from a gallery in Paris, and the ceiling-size light fixture was created with overscale red tassels from my collection for Samuel & Sons. The elegant sliding screen is from the original design by Hirsch Bedner (above, top). Famed art critic Dave Hickey attracted a remarkable group of artists to Las Vegas when he was a professor at the University of Nevada. One of my favorites is Japanese artist Sush Machida. He used a traditional wave motif, inspired by a Japanese woodcut, to create this dazzling wall-size painting that focuses the dining experience at the Robitayaki Bar. I commissioned a pair of these wonderful works for the restaurant (above, bottom).

I wanted something to focus the foreground of the view within this covered driveway entry to the Encore Boston Harbor. I found this heroically scaled polished-steel disk by British artist David Haber. Not only does it frame the view of the Mystic River beyond, but it also animates the space with delightful reflections of traffic and pedestrians (previous spread). It is entirely unexpected to find terra-cotta olive oil jars taller than the person you're standing next to, walls made of black, rounded pebbles, and ceilings adorned with coils of rope and handblown wineglasses that are four feet tall. The floors and bar top at the Teatro Ristorante at the Wynn Macau are accented with stone mosaics created in Italy, and a curved blue wall features copper repoussé sea life found in a Venetian antiques shop. The railing was inspired by Matisse drawings I admire, the chairs and bar stools were inspired by Italian furniture of the 1930s. The immense floral element that defines the entry has been replaced by an abundance of live green orchids to celebrate the summer season. This particular cymbidium is my favorite flower and a signature of my interiors. I discovered the huge container in Brussels (above and right).

Designer Elsa Schiaparelli knew how to shock. Her signature fuchsia was often combined with black-and-white stripes to extraordinarily dramatic affect. The Society Restaurant at the Wynn Encore Las Vegas was inspired by her. Centered on a giant Schiaparelli pink banquette, with leaf-green chinoiserie lanterns and dramatic black-and-white patterns on the eccentrically draped fabric and the floor, we created an active, animated space for breakfast, lunch, and dinner (above and opposite, top and bottom). Floor-to-ceiling mirrors framed with hand-beaded embroidery in Chinese cloud patterns, a partnership with Samuel & Sons, and center-mounted-elongated custom-brass and silk light sconces flank these double-sculpted doorways at the entry to a large guest suite at the Wynn Palace Cotai. Matching main bedrooms are to the left and right. I covered all the interior window frames with polished chrome to emphasize the dramatic view of the dancing waters in the world-famous fountains below (following spread).

At the Encore Boston Harbor Garden Bar and Garden Restaurant, sweeping curved edges accented with a glass and brass railing overlook the atrium beyond and its trees, flower beds, and floral-covered carousel. Large lattice, backlit chandeliers, based on the shape of French parasols, circle the white columns that embrace the curved escalators used to access these rooms. Only Steve Wynn presents design opportunities for this scale of magic. I mirrored as many surfaces as I could to capture reflections of this amazing combination of space and detail (opposite and below).

Steve Wynn broke the cardinal rule of gaming design with the Mirage, bringing daylight into and around the casino. At the Wynn Encore Las Vegas, a vaulted lattice conservatory ceiling covers this large atrium, and the tented pavilions within it contain baccarat and high-limit games of chance and edges the main area of casino play. The marble floors and pathways are inlaid with Italian glass mosaic butterfly designs from my drawings; post lighting sits atop octagonal grilled enclosures, which artfully conceal the air venting for this garden space. It took more than three years to collect the aloe bonsai trees, as we slowly gathered these extraordinary specimens in southern California and Florida. I particularly love the contrast between the almost prehistoric shapes of the plants and the sophistication of the lacquered mahogany, cut-crystal lighting, and handmade carpeting in the rooms within. Most of our guests have never encountered anything like these magnificent examples of ancient flora. They always look to me like something the dinosaurs would have eaten (left and above).

Multiple layers of design elements ensure continual surprise. This lounge area, near a concierge desk at the Wynn Encore Las Vegas, is so dense with detail that guests still discover new elements on their fourth or fifth visit. The marble tabletops have inlaid mother-of-pearl flowers, while contrasting drapery lining is seen behind two layers of tassels in mirrored reflection; enormous silk tassel tiebacks feature crystal balls and moss fringe. Guest telephones are brushed-steel reproductions of the black Bakelite original of the 1930s and were created custom for the hotel. Every chair and pillow features a different silk cord trim. The chandeliers are strung with sand-frosted beach glass pendants (previous spread). There is no glazing in the mullions of this restaurant facade at the Encore Boston Harbor, allowing the action in the corridor and the bar to mix. A ceiling of brick barrel vaults and cove lighting creates a warm feeling. Five different graphic designs of Portuguese tile collide on the floor. Hand-stitched leather seating and an antique Wurlitzer jukebox combine contemporary design and once-upon-a-time memories to create a new and exciting place to relax, meet friends, or go on the hunt. Multiple mirrored surfaces make for increased visual action and coy observation (below and opposite, top and bottom).

A tiled ceiling of beveled metro tiles in a herringbone pattern, a floor of marble inlaid terrazzo, striped with brushed brass and stainless steel, a curved bar of a rare Italian marble with a bolted-bronze light trough overhead, and cracked porcelain textured walls all work together to frame a giant installation of a fish swimming in a mirror made entirely of seashells by Thomas Boog, the Parisian master of *coquillage*. The unexpected combination of these materials and textures makes for a memorable experience at the Oyster Bar at the Encore Boston Harbor (opposite and above). For over five years, I collected forty-nine of these rare, magnificent, and unique carved dragon mirrors by the French genius Viradot, made during the late nineteenth-century reign of Napoleon III. They are prime examples of chinoiserie decorative arts, and I thought they would be the perfect complement to this casino restaurant in Southeast Asia, where dragons portend good luck by chasing away evil. All these prized examples of the pinnacle of French chinoiserie were created in lacquered mahogany. For the Wynn Palace Cotai Fontana Restaurant, I had them gold-leafed to increase their value to our Asian guests—and it made them look richer as well (following spread).

COMFORT

Steve's number one rule was to always think like a guest.

That means designing spaces that give people emotional sustenance and pleasure, but it also means anticipating their needs, and making them comfortable. It's hard to appreciate beauty if you're not comfortable.

To think like a guest, we created countless narratives of how they would use the room. How would they enter? Would they have a coat? A drink? A nice place to wait for a minute? This was especially important for the guest rooms. Just consider the act of unpacking your luggage. Is there a stable spot for your luggage to rest? Is that spot well lit? Is it convenient to the closet? And so on.

To test out these narratives, we built models of every guest room and every suite. We had to prove that everything we did was comfortable, that we'd really considered the comfort of every conceivable guest. And we didn't stop there: Steve insisted on sitting in every single chair and every single sofa. Our dining chairs, for instance, had to be comfortable for at least two and a half hours. If you installed a sofa, it had to be the right height and depth,

so it wasn't hard to get out of, even if you were seated in the middle. And if the guest was sitting on a couch, and he had a cocktail, where would he place his drink? If she was watching a screen, is the screen at the right height? Comfort isn't just a soft seat. It's getting every little detail just right.

My obsession with comfort is deeply informed by design history. I'm convinced that the first time humans were truly comfortable was the eighteenth century, with the French invention of the armchair and the sofa and the functional mattress. Once you discover that history, and begin to appreciate their ingenuity, you start to get a little competitive. How can I make it better? How can I make the sofa even more comfortable? Can I improve on the lounge chair? Can I design the best hotel bed? Because that's not just about a nice mattress and soft sheets. It's also about getting the reading light right, and making sure they can charge their devices, and easily control the blinds, and so on.

Too often, we associate luxury with expensive surfaces.

But I believe that comfort is the essence of luxury.

     aking dining a complete pleasure is no easy task. You must have the right size table at the perfect
height, comfortable and supportive chairs with enough room above the arms to clear the table,
engaging views in all directions, and flattering lighting that's also functional. We accomplished
this at the Encore Boston Harbor Red 8 Restaurant. It is equally important to make staff functions as effortless
as possible, allowing the maximum efficiency of service with the least amount of hustle and bustle to distract
the guest (page 118). In China, red is the color of luck, luxury, and wealth. These luxurious suites at the Wynn
Encore Macau with cinnabar-colored carpeting and custom wall covering were instantly sought after. But the
perfectly proportioned seating, including a return on the sofa so that one could recline while watching television,
or gazing at the spectacular view, along with considerately placed and warm tone lighting also made the suites
deeply comfortable (previous spread). I always wanted our guests to feel like they had arrived at their own
personal apartment. The reception lounge at the Wynn Las Vegas Tower Suites was no different, which is why
we furnished it like a luxurious living room. One seating area featured a rare Indo Portuguese secretaire covered
in camel bone, decorated with scenic pen-work and a pair of exceptional Ming dynasty Guan Yin carvings. An
adjacent conversation group overlooks the spacious bar (left and above). When you furnish two thousand guest
rooms at a time, it's important to get it right. That's why we always built a full-scale working model of every
proposed design. I furnished this model for the Wynn Las Vegas Resort just before my retirement. When changing
decor, I like to contrast the coloring from the previous one. This scheme would have replaced a very pale cream
room with all neutral tones. Dark walls contrasted with the light carpet would feel like a dramatic change to our
returning guests. The overscale painting made everything in the room feel intimate (following spread).

Men do not like sharing sofas, so this large lounge area for relaxing after a workout or anticipating a massage is furnished with generously scaled club chairs at the spa at the Wynn Las Vegas. Healthy snacks and beverages are available on the large credenza, and the newest issue of your favorite newspaper is offered on each giant ottoman. Light sources are located at lower locations with table lamps so that reading is as easy as snoozing or viewing media (opposite and below). This conversation area in a large two-bedroom suite at the Wynn Macau has enough seating for four guests with invited friends. Convenient tables for snacks and drinks are always within reach, and the lighting can be adjusted for any task, whether it's reading, working, intimate conversation, or watching your favorite movie. I accessorized the coffee tables with objects I would like to find in my own home, but left side tabletops free for books, cocktails, or nibbles. The large botanical drawing came from my sketchbook and is embroidered in silver metallic thread on chocolate-brown silk. The original installation of this suite design was accomplished in ninety days (following spread).

I always want to make the guests feel like they have checked into a lavish suite. This bathroom at the Wynn Encore Macau features a double lavatory counter with a center area for makeup and easily positioned seating. The counter height has been raised to prevent water from splashing on guests. The lighting was designed to allow total facial visibility with wall sconces located at the sides of the face to fill in any shadows created by the functional downlights from above. Flattery will get you everywhere. The under-counter lighting thoughtfully illuminates towels and accessory offerings during the day and can be selected to remain on during the night to guide guests into the bathroom without abrasive lights shining in their eyes—a standard design detail of Wynn Resorts (opposite). All Wynn resorts hotels have separate elevator access within the tower for resort guest rooms, or for the Tower Suites. This resort guest room at the Wynn Encore Macau is designed like a suite with separate areas for sleeping, lounging, and dining. The television in the center alcove swivels 180 degrees to be viewed from the separate seating area or bed and is opposite the floor-to-ceiling views of the South China Sea (below).

S pace in the bathroom for two people is a great luxury. In addition, perfect lighting is crucial to both function and enjoyment, which is why we engage in extensive lighting testing. Opposite the tall chest of drawers on the left in this Wynn Macau Club Suite bathroom is an ample closet in a carpeted dressing area, with every need anticipated, including, as always, an enclosed room for the commode. A dramatic setting for the two-person soaking bathtub creates possibilities that guests could never enjoy at home (below). Obviously, the bed is the most important component in a hotel bedroom. For two years we tested every possible mattress, feather pillow combination, and linen weave to arrive at the Wynn Bed for the Wynn Macau Club Suite bedroom. Oprah Winfrey called it the most comfortable bed she had ever experienced. Vertical edges on furnishings near the bed should be rounded and soft. This way, guests negotiating a new bedroom in dim lighting are never in danger (opposite, top). This seating area in our smallest suite offers comfort to accommodate any task—working, dining, reading, conversation, or relaxing. All room ceilings are at least a foot taller than most hotel guest rooms, and I bring lighting and the feeling of increased space into the room with a beamed and mirrored ceiling that holds functional downlights to create an illusion of great height. I like to use coffee tables with curved edges to make access to seating and movement around the room as easy as possible, even by moonlight (opposite, bottom).

This lounge at the Wynn Las Vegas is used by high-limit slots players who want to take a break for refreshments or by guests who are waiting for them during their play. The lounge seating group brings the planting and coloring of the adjacent garden into the space to blur the line between inside and outside. The large comfortable chairs swivel so that couples can face one another over a snack table or turn to enjoy the garden and fountain views in the walled landscape. The tables, chairs, and carpeting were all specifically designed for this unique space (previous spread). Tower Suites guests at the Encore Boston Harbor can relax while waiting for friends or a limousine, or just gather for conversation and a snack and cocktail. An antique Peruvian mirror found in Amsterdam floats over an eighteenth-century French tapestry to center one of the dramatic seating groups. The chandelier in the coffer above, like most lighting elements in this hotel, is made of handblown Murano glass. The in-house floral department changes the flower arrangements often, so that returning guests are charmed by new designs (above). At the Wynn Palace Cotai high-limit games lounge, the floral on lattice brass wall elements were inspired by a minaudière created by Van Cleef & Arpels in the 1920s that I encountered at the Musée des Arts Décoratifs in Paris, one of my favorite museums. The Metropolitan Museum of Art's beautiful collection of Chinese porcelains inspired the carpet design. The large lounge chairs with white lacquer arms took inspiration from a pair of Shanghai art deco armchairs I saw in Los Angeles. The eighteenth-century Italian mirror over the center consul was found at an antiques gallery in Florence. And the chandelier was enlarged from a 1930s example by the Venetian architect Carlo Scarpa. The red lacquer cocktail tables resemble an item I saw in a Christie's auction. Traveling the world enables one to bring together an eclectic set of inspirations. And beauty is important, but an object must also be functional (right).

A space by my friend, the extraordinarily talented designer Todd-Avery Lenahan, inspired this elegant bathroom at the Wynn Encore Macau. He's also my successor. The spider marble for the walls and floor, a signature of Wynn Resorts, comes from a single quarry in Macedonia. Every need has been carefully considered and accommodated. In a lavish bathroom, lighting is one of the most important considerations, and in this bathroom the light can be adjusted for both close personal inspection and for steeping in a romantic bath (left and below). This corner bedroom at the Wynn Macau presents extraordinary views of the South China Sea—and a unique problem. To maximize the drama of this prime location, we needed to solve the problem of where to locate the media. We placed a pop-up television in the cabinet at the foot of the bed, which rises quietly to the right elevation for viewing. Large bedside tables hold the media control, a telephone, and a book, drink, or snack. Lighting controls on both sides of the bed can change the lighting, the drapery, and the temperature. A spot for reading with a snack and a drink is accommodated in the corner (following spread).

Today's traveler needs a lot of surface space and perfectly located electrical resources to accommodate many digital platforms. At the Wynn Palace Cotai, we make all these necessities easily available at both bedside and desktop (opposite, top). Furnishing a closet shows a guest that you really care. These walk-in closets have soft wool carpeting under foot, an adjustable three-way mirror, drawers for both folded shirts and sweaters, a leather tray to catch jewelry and coins, well-illuminated hanging rods, and easy-to-find additional bedding, such as pillows, blankets, and a throw for an afternoon nap—all essentials (opposite, bottom). The tower in the Wynn Palace Cotai was made extra-large so that each resort room could truly be a suite with separate bathroom, bedroom, and living room facilities. Floor-to-ceiling glass provides views of Cotai and the sea beyond. We addressed every possible activity in the design—from conversation to reading to working. Each of the guest rooms was given a signature color scheme inspired by an eighteenth-century enameled porcelain teacup, once owned by the emperor (above). Guests exhausted by robust play at the slot machines can gather here in the high-limit slot games lounge at the Wynn Palace Cotai to be served a restorative tea or select snacks. Heavy brocade draperies with long tassel tiebacks, and super thick carpeting ensure a quiet place away from the frenetic machines. The design of the Murano glass fixture was inspired by Asian flowers: a lotus and chrysanthemum combined. The glass is infused with 24-karat gold to warm the light and add shimmer (following spread).

LUXURY

When I was younger, all I wanted was the ability to acquire nice things.

I assumed that was the dream. But as I got older, I began to realize that with infinite choice comes confusion. It's hard knowing what you want.

This insight has shaped my thoughts on luxury. True luxury, I've come to believe, is having the best choices made for you. It's not about having a million options—it's about having someone who knows what they're doing find the best options for you. It's about creating a space that just feels right, even if you can't explain why.

As I mentioned in the comfort chapter, luxury isn't just about adding fancy and grand things. Comfort is a crucial component of luxury. That's why we wanted to make public spaces that are sophisticated and elegant, but we also didn't want to make them intimidating or exclusive. Our spaces had to feel comfortable if the man was in black tie and the woman was in a gown, but they had to be equally comfortable for the couple in jeans and t-shirts.

How did we do that? By focusing on human scale and intimacy. It's not a casino. It's your casino. It's not a dining room. It's your table. Everything should feel like it's been done just for you. That's luxury, and that's why your enjoyment of the room doesn't depend on your outfit.

Of course, luxury is also about giving guests unexpectedly elevated experiences. If you're designing a cabana, you need to provide shade and privacy. That's the bare minimum. But luxury happens when you also install two extra layers of trim around the edge, with tassels and tassel tiebacks, and a finial or five on the roof of the cabana. Luxury is discovering a game in the cabana cabinet, or a full set of glassware and china. Are those flourishes necessary? Of course not. But they elevate the cabana. They make it a luxury, a tent from *Arabian Nights*, and not just a source of shade by the pool.

The same approach informed our outdoor dining design. We set tables by a koi pond, and put them in tents. It's a lovely space. But to make it a luxurious space, we hung crystal chandeliers inside the tents. It's completely unnecessary. It feels extravagant. And that's the point.

But sometimes the most meaningful luxuries are subtle, barely noticed. In the suites at the Wynn and Encore, I had a London company that specialized in custom hand-painted and embroidered wallcoverings make one that I'd designed that was inspired by a piece of porcelain I saw in Dresden. A floating feathers motif, which was hand embroidered on Chinese silk. It was the most expensive wall covering I'd ever used and we installed it in the powder room. Not the bedroom. Not the entry. The powder room. Because luxury doesn't have to be a loud spectacle.

True luxury is a state of mind, defining the guest experience all the way down.

It's like sable lining in a raincoat—you certainly don't need it, but it sure feels nice.

One of the greatest luxuries one can have in a hotel accommodation is space. This is the guest's first view when entering one of the villas at the Wynn Palace Cotai. The double-height space looks through contemporary, chinoiserie-shaped windows to a 150-foot-long pool with laminar fountain jets and a row of trees with the South China Sea beyond. The windows are framed with hand-embroidered Rubelli satin; the upholstery was woven on hand looms in the heart of West Hollywood by Maria Kipp. Absolutely everything in this room is bespoke. This is haute couture design for living (page 146). The bar/entry of the Wing Lei Restaurant at Wynn Las Vegas presented an opportunity to open a window revealing this two-hundred-year-old pomegranate tree framed by a whimsical shaped valance with a constellation of gilded chrysanthemums mounted on a golden *capiz* shell background by Maya Romanoff. The Ming dynasty cloisonné turtles carry original earthquake detectors on their backs (previous spread). Baccarat is a game that attracts serious players. This lounge at the Wynn Las Vegas offers for players or their guests a place to relax, talk about the day's winnings, and enjoy a delicious buffet, as well as beverages, all served gratis. Elegant bathroom facilities are tucked behind the lacquered and gilded screen. An abundance of live flowers, often refreshed, adds to the feeling of luxury (below). Players wagering the most often prefer to do so away from the gaze of other guests. We accommodate them in lavish private salons like this one at the Wynn Las Vegas. If the game of your choice is not in the room, give us an hour and we will install it. There is room for your entourage to relax while they are pampered by an attentive staff. Traditionally, a formal space like this one would be designed with a single, large, central chandelier. I opted to cover the ceiling with a series of matching crystal pendants designed especially for the space. This unique lighting solution allows the gaming configuration to be changed quickly on the player's whim. Walls are paneled in lambskin parchment that I developed with Townsend leather specifically for the project (opposite).

We began thinking of the design for the Wynn Palace Cotai at the same time Steve asked me to redesign this extraordinary restaurant, Wing Lei, at the Wynn Las Vegas. It features fine Asian cuisine by a world-renowned chef who Steve lured from Hong Kong. I invented this beautiful handmade wall covering with Maya Romanoff and elongated my wall sconce design for Boyd Lighting to distinguish the new spaces. The creator of our crystal dragon sculpted these chrysanthemums and finished them in gold leaf over a red lacquer base. The lanterns were created for the room, as were the embroidered chair backs. Fromental of London created the hand-painted gold tea paper used to cover movable screens to divide the space for private dining. The room came alive when we found the emerald green stemware for the tables (previous spread). Famed Parisian designer Jacques Garcia created the original interiors for Wing Lei at the Wynn Las Vegas. The huge vase-shaped niches in the room and the ceiling configuration were his design. I selected a favorite Venetian glass chandelier for the space, originally designed by John Hutton. Maya Romanoff created the gold tea paper between the four giant urns, and we arranged a constellation of golden chrysanthemums within the white lacquered voids of the urn silhouettes. Green lacquer for the entry doors ensured a dramatic reveal (opposite). The entry to Wing Lei in Las Vegas is a hundred feet away from the Tower Suites guest reception. My version of a traditional Ming dynasty frog beam was used to center a pair of doors that beckon guests to enter. Crystals from the original chandeliers in this restaurant now pour from a golden dragon's mouth into large porcelain vases. I call this luxury recycling. The tassels, custom colored to resemble the best jade, were inspired by a four-inch-high key tassel, which was enlarged to three feet by the masters of passementerie, Samuel & Sons (below). The main dining room and bar at Wing Lei at the Wynn Las Vegas look out on a private garden with two-hundred-year-old pomegranate trees and a golden dragon sculpture that holds a huge onyx pearl. I collected every sample I could find of gold on white wall covers and then I tried to select a single pattern to cover the ceilings and the walls. The answer was not which one to use. The answer was to use all of them. This is a favorite solution to a design question when presented with a lavish selection. Not one—all (following spread)!

I like guests to gasp when they turn a corner. Lavish use of tieback drapery allowed me to achieve this desired
effect and to quiet the corridor, which provides access to the most personal beauty services and relaxing
massages, at the Encore Boston Harbor spa (opposite, top). My successor, Todd-Avery Lenahan, designed
a room like this in our Las Vegas property. Convinced nothing could be better, I recolored it for inclusion in the
Encore Boston Harbor. The photo is shown with all the lights on. When the lighting is dimmed, this is a space
of contemplative comfort and relaxation (opposite, bottom). This is a version of another extraordinary space
designed by Todd-Avery Lenahan. In every resort, I asked the most talented people I knew to create "cameo
appearances," and Todd participated in every project. This version was adapted and recolored for the Encore
Boston Harbor, but the promise of pure luxury and glamour beautifully delivered is all Todd (above). This lavish
and luxurious bathroom at the Wynn Las Vegas is hers and hers alone. Each master bedroom of the villas boasted
this extravagant private space, as well as an equally extravagant masculine version. All the cabinets, including
the closets, are lacquered faux ivory to frame inset sections of mirror. The countertops and bath surround are
rare honey-veined onyx, as is the shower and commode compartment behind the doors. Luxury is not an infinite
number of choices. Luxury is having all the right choices made for you (following spread).

Convention areas and meeting rooms can often be the most boring and utilitarian spaces in a hotel. We wanted to change that. We started by giving every meeting room at the Wynn Las Vegas an extraordinary view. Walls are upholstered in a custom fabric by the Italian house of Rubelli, providing the perfect hush to a congested room. The chandeliers, inspired by fanciful parasols, feature rock-crystal pendants. The linens have been hand-embroidered, the china designed for the space, and the finest crystal and silverware are typical of this elevated level of hospitality. Even the media in the space is concealed in the ceiling, designed to be revealed with the touch of a button. Every meeting room in this resort features an outside terrace, extending the experience into the landscape beyond (below and opposite). This is the men's whirlpool and cold plunge at the Encore Boston Harbor spa. Rooms that are often wet require special consideration. Floors must be beautiful but not slippery. Every surface must stand up to chlorinated liquids. Heated chaise longues have tables within easy reach for a restorative beverage or snack. Towels are available in abundance and thoughtfully placed. Even the handrail deserves careful design consideration. All the lighting is indirect, so that it never shines in the eyes of a relaxing guest. The wall most out of harm's way is draped in heavy, stainproof velvet to dampen acoustics and prevent echo. Air is refreshed with a clean masculine sent (following spread).

These cabanas at the Wynn Encore have been designed to serve both daytime sun worshippers and nighttime party people. Bleach cleanable upholstery is flipped from dayside to nightside to ensure that tanning oils do not stain evening clothes. Ample countertops hold daytime refreshments and snacks, as well as bottle service during nightclub hours. Lighting can be adjusted from very bright to very low. Ceiling fans provide a welcome breeze in sunny Las Vegas and concealed water vapor nozzles cool the air day or night (opposite and below). The private pool at Bartolotta Ristorante di Mare in Las Vegas is alive with brightly colored koi and papyrus reeds. Guests enjoy the finest Italian cuisine poolside under tented cabanas with crystal chandeliers or loggias with custom lanterns. The flagstone mosaic wall enclosing the cabana and service area was inspired by a texture I noticed from a car in the countryside above Florence, while traveling thirty-five miles an hour. It might be better than the actual wall; my memories and impressions often are (following spread).

Every villa in a Wynn resort has a private dining room. This lavish example at the Wynn Encore Macau is perfect in every way except one. Asian guests prefer round tables with a lazy Susan for gathering with family and guests. Even though the table and the chairs were created bespoke for this room, they did not function as well as I would've liked. Mistakes are important teachers (left). This foyer and the hallway beyond lead to a single large bedroom, a powder room, and a private spa at the Wynn Encore Macau. Italian mosaics on the foyer floor are acoustically foiled by thick padded panels upholstered in cocoa-colored mohair plush with Swarovski crystal buttons. The Murano chandelier overhead and shaded table lamps provide a soft ambience (above). The generously scaled floral motifs on the carpeting in the reception area at the Wynn Palace Cotai match the mosaic floors of the adjacent conservatory. Horizontal bands of a rare emerald green marble face the reception, concierge, and bellman desks. Table lamps divide personal functions and provide flattering sidelight sources for guests and staff alike. The polished-steel sculptures along the red lacquered wall are large-scale versions of traditional Chinese artifacts created by artist Liao Yibai that I found in a Manhattan gallery. The artist probes questions of cultural value: Are the objects more valuable because they are large and shiny? Or less valuable because they are new? As at all Wynn properties, the botanical designs are changed often to provide variety for returning guests, and to respond to holidays and the seasons (following spread).

ENTERTAINMENT

One of the reasons people visit Las Vegas is that entertainment can happen anytime, anywhere.

Entertainment is not just the show in the theater—it's the games. It's the food. It's the shopping and people watching. From a design perspective, that means we have to provide venues for entertainment throughout the hotel. And it's only gotten harder, since our entertainment now has to compete with that phone in your pocket.

Consider the race and sports book room. In 2005, we opened with state-of-the-art technology. By 2015, the room was woefully out of date, and not just because the televisions had gotten bigger and brighter. The entire point of the room had changed, as it was no longer enough to just put a comfortable chair in front of a screen. Now we needed places where VIPs could entertain their guests. We needed a place for very serious and studious bettors—they needed a desk with several screens, plus lighting for reading, but we also couldn't make it feel like an office. We also needed a space for groups to gather and have a drink. It's just one big room, but it has to entertain different people in very different ways.

Sometimes you don't know what people want from a room until you build it. Our first nightclub at the Wynn had private rooms for celebrities. But it didn't quite work. And then we realized that people didn't want privacy at the club, even if they said they did. They really wanted to be together at the coolest party in town. So we made the coolest living room. We built an underlit onyx floor, with over a thousand lampshade light fixtures floating above. The system was designed so that we never had to repeat any of the lighting effects—there are infinite possibilities of color and pattern. You need lighting, but just because you need it doesn't mean it can't be part of the entertainment.

But entertainment isn't just about the amusement of the guests. You also need to serve the staff, and make sure the space makes service as effortless as possible. Does the staff have a clear path between the guests and the bar and the kitchen? Can they see what they're doing?

One of my challenges is televisions. I hate televisions. I don't like their light, or their moving images, or the way they distract people. But they're obviously necessary in some spaces. So the question is: how do you frame them? If you want to watch the screen, I want to ensure it's comfortable—the television should be the right size and at the right angle. But if you're not there to watch, I want to help you avoid the distraction. I want you to be able to enjoy all the other types of entertainment in the room.

Above all, an entertaining space is one where people can see each other. It's watching other people at the club, but also at the gaming tables and the restaurants and the gardens. It's creating a room where everyone feels good and looks good.

We're social animals— watching other people is the ultimate entertainment.

For the first time in the company's history, we designed a double-level casino— for the Encore Boston Harbor. We took advantage of the height to create private gaming salons on the upper level, giving each a French balcony from which guests could enjoy the view over the activity below. Each salon was carefully considered with lounging and dining facilities for the players as well as their entourage. The custom carpeting is the same as in the baccarat rooms of the Wynn Las Vegas, so guests don't forget their host (page 174). Baccarat is the highest stakes game and so the rooms for play must be very opulent. Cascades of cut-velvet draperies framed by tall folding screens of white lacquer and carved gold-leafed wood against lambskin parchment walls establish a luxe atmosphere at the Wynn Las Vegas. A sculpture by contemporary artist Timothy Horn was inspired by a brooch worn by a European empress (previous spread). Boston is a sports town. This comfortable men's-club-style restaurant at the Encore Boston Harbor invites Bostonians to enjoy their favorite sporting event on large televisions while they enjoy elevated versions of American TV snacks. In today's world, sports entertainment is a twenty-four-hour event, and this intimate space is filled with fans all day and night. Old leather belts became a horizontal textured wall cover to reinforce the old club feel. We tested both the Spanish armchairs and the Belgian bar stools for hours to be sure that they would provide the comfort required for a long sporting match or even back-to-back games (above and opposite, top and bottom).

B etting on sporting events has been a Las Vegas tradition since gaming was legalized. New technology requires fast adaptation. The high-definition video screens overhead replaced a similar installation that was less than ten years old at the Wynn Las Vegas. Every chair has a tilt and swivel function for maximum comfort and an adjacent table for the attentive snack and beverage service. Guests sometimes stay for six to eight hours. Desks are positioned for those who are tracking their bets or reading complimentary racing forms. Private VIP boxes can be engaged for groups who want to enjoy the sporting action together. This is one of the most electrically charged rooms on earth during the Super Bowl, with every seat reserved long in advance (previous spread). Shortly after we opened our first resort in Macau, Steve Wynn asked me to invent a new nightclub. I was given forty-five days to pull off the Wynn Macau Nightclub at the Cinnabar. Fortunately, I had just refurbished the suites in Las Vegas. Their lounge chairs and sofas, already upholstered in a durable red fabric, were cleaned, restored, and flown to China, accompanied by several of my red lacquered mirror designs, to which I added an array of votive candles. All the walls were draped with an iridescent and flame-retardant copper-colored taffeta. The carpet design was in my sketchbook and was ordered immediately. I found a supplier of mirrored disco balls and bought their entire stock. The balls for the centerpiece above the dance floor joined the chairs and sofas for their transoceanic flights (below and opposite).

N ightclubs changed the entertainment component of Las Vegas forever. Guests no longer wanted dinner and a show. They wanted a late dinner and to be the show. This space, Tryst, at the the Wynn Las Vegas, had the advantage of a preexisting sixty-five-foot-tall waterfall cascading into a large pool. Almost overnight, we invented an indoor/outdoor nightclub. Inside was a cinematic blaze of red patent alligator banquettes, red draperies, red carpeting, lacquer red walls, a red ceiling, and red lighting. This entire interior was designed and completed in ninety days. The red velvet drapery was the final touch, framing the extraordinary vista of the waterfall from the entrance: instant disco inferno (previous spread). A view of XS at the Encore Las Vegas, one of the most successful nightclubs in Las Vegas history. The entertainment is provided by world-class DJs and by the guests, who dance on every surface (below). Blush, a nightclub at the Wynn Las Vegas: another ninety-day wonder. My design partner, Janellen Radoff, told Steve Wynn that he had always made us jump through hoops but now he was lighting them on fire. Sean Christie was a young nightclub talent when Steve engaged him to turn a failing nightspot into one of the most successful in Las Vegas. With Sean's direction, we created this sexy living room on top of the underlit onyx dance floor of the previous club (right). XS became the place to be seen in Las Vegas—it was so popular that it could not accommodate everyone who wanted to participate in the nighttime reverie. The pool, with its sunburst tile design, was the center of outdoor nightlife (following spread).

These luxe, curved, leather upholstered banquettes at XS in Las Vegas are where I sat with Bette Midler one memorable night. We mirrored every surface of the traditional chandelier shape just like the spherical disco balls that created the tradition. The large floor lamps become dance poles for guests. Every surface was designed to be danced on: seating, tables, and occasionally even the walls (opposite)! The Surrender nightclub and the beach club beyond replaced the original porte cochere entry at the Wynn Encore on the Las Vegas Strip. The huge serpent behind the bar was inspired by my first thought for a name for this club: Original Sin, a nod to Adam and Eve. I often invented design concepts during my early morning swims. During one productive session, I wondered what it would be like to combine chrome yellow upholstery and leopard carpeting with brushed stainless steel. This is the result. An entire movable glass wall joins the energy of the club to the energy of the vast pool area beyond, creating one of the most popular nighttime venues in Vegas (below).

The casino has always been the preeminent form of entertainment for visitors to Las Vegas and now to Macau. The Wynn Encore Macau is the smallest and most exclusive casino in our repertoire. The gold-infused glass chandeliers above the gaming tables were commissioned on the island of Murano. They are not a light source as much as they are a definition of the ambience of the space. The handmade carpets scattered with imaginary flowers are deep and rich. The curve in the center of the casino increases the intimacy of the space. There are no long vistas here—only intimate gatherings. The mango yellow linen walls are covered with figures in silk soutache and Swarovski crystal appliqués. The seating was designed specifically for the space and features a favorite Rubelli silk damask with a fuchsia cord edge (left). We create large working models of every casino space. This looks exactly like the casino at the Wynn Palace in Cotai, but it is actually a model built in Las Vegas. I changed chairs, drapery, lighting fixtures, and carpeting several times before we arrived at the perfect combination. Getting this stage set exactly right is crucial. Every detail is deeply considered, from the embroidery to the handles on the backs of the baccarat chairs. The large chandelier was made by master craftsmen in Murano and inspired by Asian flowers (above).

We quickly outgrew the original poker room in the sister hotel, Wynn Las Vegas. The new and much larger facility at the Wynn Encore was designed to include a high-limit games area. Friendly curved corners created with leather-covered panels embrace the room. Lighting is crucial in a poker room. Players need to see their cards and the other players' faces perfectly. Is there a tell at the table? It is no accident that every member of our lighting design team came from the theater (previous spread). Gaming has become a more dynamic activity. This room at the Wynn Encore in Las Vegas features not only games of chance but also foosball and other games to amuse and relax ardent players. Donghia, a brand usually found only in upscale homes, was selected for all the lounge furniture to add residential elegance. My distinctive design for the twenty-one stools was lacquered white with cobalt blue chenille upholstery, Steve Wynn's favorite color (below). Loyalty programs have become a very successful marketing device for casinos. Red Card members are rewarded for play with merchandise, hotel rooms, and food and beverage. This lounge at the Wynn Palace Cotai lets guests make their choices alone at an interactive digital table screen, or in consultation with a staff member at one of the luxurious conversation groups where they can also enjoy a beverage (opposite, top). Everything in this room at the Wynn Encore Macau is defined by luxury: the handmade carpet on the floor, extravagant armchairs with Italian cut-velvet backs, mango silk walls embroidered by the team that creates gowns for Oscar de la Renta, hand-carved wall sconces, and silk shaded Venetian chandeliers that are backlit to provide the most flattering illumination (opposite, bottom). People-watching is one of my favorite forms of entertainment. This bar, the Parasol Up Lounge at the Wynn Las Vegas, is in the heart of the resort and almost every seat has a prime view of the circulation areas. Guests on the banquettes in the center of the room can hide away for an intimate conversation. The polished-chrome ball at the center of the bar animates the room as guests come and go. The colorful Axminster carpet is from my sketchbook. The modern Italian chairs by Rubelli have backs upholstered in my favorite fabric, Rubelli's Modern Art cut-velvet brocade, which was originally produced in the 1920s (following spread).

JOY

When I think of joy, I think of a space that's ready for a celebration.

This doesn't mean you throw confetti on the floor, but it does mean that the space feels fit for a party.

How does one do that? It starts with color. The palette of joyous colors is really the palette of flowers. I'm reminded of Matisse here—his color schemes reverberate with the same sort of joy you get from a field of wildflowers in the sun. I have yet to see a depressing Matisse.

When I think of designing for joy, I often think about the atrium at the Wynn. When Steve first walked into the atrium, he told me that something was off—the trunks of the trees were too gray. So we painted the trees brown with a non-toxic milk-based paint. But the construction dust had also caused these matured ficuses to defoliate. To fix that, we installed silk leaves throughout the canopy to give them that sense of abundance that's crucial to joy. But Steve said he wanted flowers in the trees.

At first, I didn't know how to do that. But then I remembered being ten years old at Gump's department store in San Francisco. They had this display with floating balls overflowing with silk flowers that were woven into an elaborate lattice. This was a week before we opened, and I began working with the flower department on the install. We had to use fire retardant Styrofoam balls, but we filled them with multiple types of flowers in a variety of bright, Matisse-like colors. I honestly didn't know if they'd work, but they've since become a signature element of the Wynn. We'd always had a surfeit of live flowers at ground level—I often used extravagant bouquets to announce the entrance to a restaurant or a room—but those floating balls suffused joy throughout the entire space.

We even brought that exuberant sense of joy to the floor, which features these overscaled floral elements. They're not literal designs, but are filled with evocative patterns, and ensure that no matter where you're looking you're enveloped in bright, joyful colors. I want you to feel as if you've walked into a Matisse painting.

Joy can also be found in the little things. There's something celebratory about a properly done table setting. For the Sinatra Restaurant and Bar, I had dragonflies embroidered on all the napkins. We had a garden view for the room, and butterflies everywhere else, but I wanted this setting to be a little surprising. We got a similar effect by placing green orchids in Murano glass vases at every table, and by using hand-cut crystal glasses at our more economical restaurants. Joy is not about doing enough. It's about going beyond.

Joy is also about reconnecting people to their childhood, and that childlike sense of wonder. We do this with our elaborate Christmas decorations, which feature these Lilliputian villages, but also with our public displays of moving carousels, Ferris wheels, and hot air balloons covered in bright flowers. I've always said that our designs should have a "once upon a time" quality, that they should contain an element of the fantastical and the cinematic. That quality gives you the freedom to experience joy—you've stepped away from ordinary life—but they also evoke a sense of nostalgia.

You are five years old again, transfixed for a moment by something beautiful and strange.

An abundance of colorful flowers always makes me joyful. Two decades ago I went to the Aalsmeer flower market near Amsterdam with a flower broker who introduced to me by legendary master of flowers Jeffrey Leatham. His selections of the very best at this world source market (which supplies 80 percent of the world's cut flowers) were flown weekly to our hotels in Las Vegas. Each hotel had an in-house floral staff. Together with the floral studio, we created distinctive arrangements, changing them often to delight and surprise returning guests. These arrangements grace the reception area of the Wynn Macau (page 200). A pair of costly curved escalators embracing a beautiful bar brings guests to restaurants on the lower lakeside level of the atrium center of the Wynn Las Vegas. This ballet of parasols, suspended above the escalators and bar, frames the view of the Lake of Dreams water feature. When I conceived the idea for this area, the name for this resort was Le Revè (The Dream). These parasols change elevation and rotate very slowly. The festival of colors is repeated in the floor coverings. I drew the embroidery patterns on the parasols in one session, behind closed doors, listening to my favorite music (previous spread). If flowers are joyful, then a floral-covered carousel and hot air balloon are Joy^2. We called on my dear friend and event impresario Preston Bailey to create these kinetic fantasy works in the Wynn Las Vegas atrium. Conceiving joyful moments like these is one thing; building them, another. A second friend, Scott Acton, invented the construction technique, and employed a small army of art students to pavé the forms with silk botanicals and jewels (above and right).

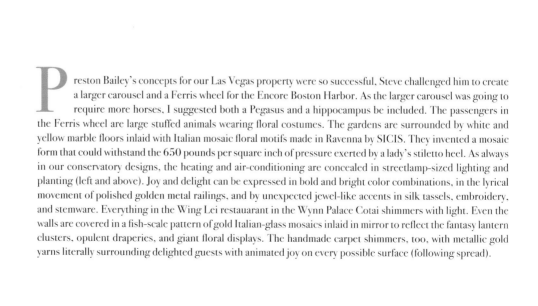

Preston Bailey's concepts for our Las Vegas property were so successful, Steve challenged him to create a larger carousel and a Ferris wheel for the Encore Boston Harbor. As the larger carousel was going to require more horses, I suggested both a Pegasus and a hippocampus be included. The passengers in the Ferris wheel are large stuffed animals wearing floral costumes. The gardens are surrounded by white and yellow marble floors inlaid with Italian mosaic floral motifs made in Ravenna by SICIS. They invented a mosaic form that could withstand the 650 pounds per square inch of pressure exerted by a lady's stiletto heel. As always in our conservatory designs, the heating and air-conditioning are concealed in streetlamp-sized lighting and planting (left and above). Joy and delight can be expressed in bold and bright color combinations, in the lyrical movement of polished golden metal railings, and by unexpected jewel-like accents in silk tassels, embroidery, and stemware. Everything in the Wing Lei restauarant in the Wynn Palace Cotai shimmers with light. Even the walls are covered in a fish-scale pattern of gold Italian-glass mosaics inlaid in mirror to reflect the fantasy lantern clusters, opulent draperies, and giant floral displays. The handmade carpet shimmers, too, with metallic gold yarns literally surrounding delighted guests with animated joy on every possible surface (following spread).

S teve Wynn wanted our guests to enter the Wynn Las Vegas resort surrounded by a fantasy atrium. Two weeks before we opened, walking through the gardens, Steve and Elaine Wynn both felt that the canopies of the trees lacked interest. I invented the flower-covered spheres hanging from the branches with our floral department and tried a few test pieces for Steve and Elaine's approval. Fortunately, there were forty-seven florists in the hotel's flower studio, and working overtime they completed nearly a hundred of these large single-color balls of flowers to dance above the heads of our guests among the foliage in time for the opening. Here's another secret: Steve did not like the gray color of the trunks and branches of the giant specimen ficus trees. Our botanical department located a milk-based paint, and the structures of the trees were painted in a warm brown in the weeks before the opening gala (above and right).

I found a pair of giant Sicilian crystal-beaded urns made in the late nineteenth century at a Christie's auction in New York—just the thing to bring delight to the center of the food displays of this large buffet restaurant with views of the extraordinary fountain show beyond at the Wynn Palace Cotai. The beads are a frozen reflection of the water drops beyond. These unexpected light sources combined with the array of fantasy lanterns above created a room of wonder for guests while selecting delicious nibbles from the artful displays that covered these polished black granite surfaces (opposite and below). I always have joyful experiences in flower shops and candy stores, so we combined the two to create the entrance to Fontana, a twenty-four-hour dining experience at the Wynn Palace Cotai. Again, Joy². Color elicits joy for me and particularly in the paintings of Henri Matisse. His adventurous palette was the basis for everything we did in combining chinoiserie with sophisticated colors for this delightful experience (following spread).

In the Wynn Palace Cotai Garden Villa Bar and Dining, our garden villas are the most extraordinary guest accommodations on the planet. I like to think of the bar and dining areas as places of possibility, where guests can gather to celebrate friendship and love or to mark special events. Hand-crafted carpeting, embroidered silks, cut velvet, and the finest furniture all combine to create truly sumptuous party places. Each of these rooms at the Wynn Palace Cotai has a balcony overlooking the main living room space with polished-brass railings adorned with rare onyx spheres (opposite, top and bottom). Each rooftop villa at the Wynn Las Vegas is enclosed behind a wall and surrounded by a private garden. The salon is a glass box set apart from the rest of the villa centered within the landscape, pool, and terraces. The luxe, handmade carpet has no fewer than seven different kinds of wool and silk and even includes a texture of woven shoelaces. The painting, one of a pair by San Francisco artist Charley Brown, was inspired by brightly colored fans fluttering in a garden (below).

I first created the palette and vocabulary for this restaurant at our Wynn Las Vegas Resort. It was so popular that we brought it to our first hotel in China, the Wynn Macau. The shocking pink and mango yellow color scheme is what I call "festival evocative"—a party waiting to happen. Live floral plantings at the edges and the view to the landscaping at the poolside beyond the room make this garden setting the perfect place to gather for fun and play. My favorite detail has always been the custom lacquered wood shapes on the passementerie trim at the edge of the draperies. They make the sound of castanets when you brush up against them (below and right). With the entire restaurant focused on the theater of the dancing water fountains in the lake, I conceived each of the private dining areas at Wing Lei at the Wynn Palace Cotai as lavish balconies in an opera house. I have always loved the tales of dining and card playing that went on in the opera theaters of Europe in the eighteenth and nineteenth centuries. I wanted to create a space perfect for that kind of joyful gathering. The dining experience is the most important event in the space. You may remember the decorative vocabulary from the prototype of this room, the restaurant of the same name in Las Vegas. In this iteration, I followed my favorite credo: nothing succeeds like excess (following spread).

MYSTERY

Mystery is about the layers.

My goal is to create designs that are so abundant and rich a guest can return four or five times to the same space and continue to notice new elements, new features, new layers. They notice the obvious stuff on their first visit, then they see something behind that, and behind that. They probably assume those elements have been added to the room, but the reality is that those layers have always been there. It's like great literature—you can return to the same novel again and again because you're able to keep discovering new things in the old words. It's familiar, but still capable of surprise.

So how does one embed mystery into a space? The use of different scales is one effective strategy. When you combine precise details and small objets d'art with features that work on a grand scale, such as a sprawling mosaic, you make it easy for people to focus on a single layer at a time. Perhaps they notice the fine details at first. But when they return, they're able to take a step back and see the mosaic, or the pattern to the garden. The different scales become layers.

You can also create a sense of mystery with lighting. For instance, we gave the casino a mysterious mood by using a shade of light that resembled the soft glow of candlelight. We also lit the space dramatically, and with sources that were unexpected. Mirrors and reflections also connote mystery with their dancing, mercurial reflections.

I would always say in our design meetings: "We need something to make our guests scratch their heads. We need something that's not obvious, that doesn't belong here." One way we did that was with pieces no one had ever seen before. Maybe it's a large secretary that is completely covered in camel bone that has been drawn on with a pin. Or tall obelisks beaded with evening gown materials. Or a small rhino statue emerging from a large amethyst geode. Or a beautiful work of art that itself contains a mystery. These aesthetic surprises draw you in, encouraging you to engage with the space.

The same goes for tension, which arises from unexpected arrangements and layouts. It's like dissonance in music—pure consonance gets boring fast, which is why you want to inject a dose of the dissonant. For instance, we did this with asymmetrically placed chandeliers. People are so used to centered chandeliers that the lighting almost becomes invisible. But if you hang them off center, the light fixture becomes noticeable again. You scratch your head and pay attention, even if you're not sure why. Of course, I also took this strategy to its logical extreme and, in the Salon Privé at Wynn Las Vegas, had hundreds of small identical chandeliers hanging from every intersection of the wood beams.

The layering of mystery can also be literal. Layers of drapery are triggers for curiosity—we want to know what's behind them, what's being hidden. It's almost gothic. We did a room with silk drapery covering all the walls. We then placed corsages of silk flowers at random on the drapery, with another layer of drapery on top of that. Then there were tassels pulling back the drapery, along with free hanging tassels placed at random. Why were the tassels there? Why would anyone do that? That was the delightful mystery.

Beauty is related to mystery. A sense of beauty is often triggered by a kind of sensory excess—there is more here than we can perceive. There's a lovely abundance of layers, and details, and elements we want to see but can't fully take in. Which is why we return. Because there's more to discover. Because we can return to the same space and see something for the first time.

Because the mystery persists.

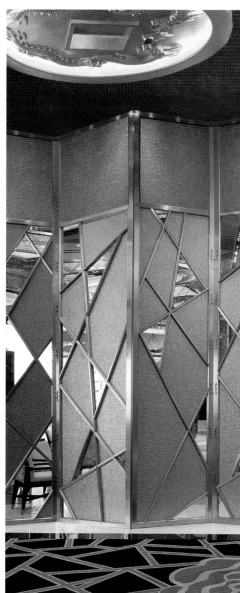

This extraordinary hallway was created to assure heightened anticipation for only two private slot playrooms at the Wynn Encore Macau. Mirrors are forbidden near card games because one cannot control the privacy of a player's hand of cards. I was able to use mirrors to my heart's content to create this truly joyous access to the most kinetic games of chance (page 222). This is a moment of truly celebratory theater, designed to usher guests into the private gaming rooms on the left and right at the Wynn Palace Cotai. A collection of high-limit card games is arrayed in the space beyond. Mirrors animate spaces because the slightest movement creates reflective energy. Here, gold tinted mirrors surround guests as they move into the rooms of play beyond. I placed the four chests in this corridor so that they could hold the eight silk lampshades at the level of the guests' faces, making everyone look their most attractive (previous spread). The reception area of the Golden Flower Restaurant at the Wynn Encore Macau, featuring the cuisine of northern China, was created specifically to serve rare tea to arriving guests. The ceiling is composed of eighty-eight illuminated glass teapots to reinforce this idea. Eight is the best number in China. Two eights are better than one. The walls were inspired by the gold-on-turquoise scheme of the Peacock Room, designed by artist James Abbott McNeill Whistler for his patron, now at the Freer Gallery in Washington, DC, one of my favorite places (opposite and below). The ceiling of the Golden Flower in Macau is covered in silk light fixtures created by the Venetian icon Mario Fortuny. It was the Venetian Marco Polo who brought Chinese culture and cuisine to his home city and to Europe. I wanted to return the favor by bringing some of Venice to China. The Fortuny pendants above the tables in the bay windows are hung from giant golden coins that signify good luck. The carpet pattern, one of my favorite Chinese design elements, is called cracked ice, and it is also auspicious. A team of embroiderers in India often used by Oscar de la Renta created the dramatically textured appliqués for the chair backs; Samuel & Sons helped me create the silk tassels strung on gold chains that cover the entire wall to the right (following spread).

O pposite the window view, nine-foot-tall screens continue the carpet pattern of cracked ice in the Golden Flower Restaurant. The screens are covered with the eponymous golden flowers—chrysanthemums—that are much honored in China. Exotic lilies are always found on each table. Perfectly colored flowers grace the gilded branches and the center table stacked with more edible goodies. Their crimson, fuchsia, and yellow coloring is the perfect complement for the room (below). The entire ceiling, including an auspicious symbol for good luck, was lacquered an orange red to match the shapes in the carpeting and the handmade vermilion wall covering for my collection for Maya Romanoff, which was created just for this room. The mosaic flowers on the entry doors came from Ravenna, and the wall sconces came from a collection I created for Niedermeyer Chicago. Again, they were conceived specifically for this private dining room at the Golden Flower. The center of the room is a cascade of smaller Mario Fortuny silk fixtures, ensuring that my favorite party city, Venice, had a presence in this private party room (opposite). This restaurant at the Wynn Palace Cotai, Red 8, has full views of the casino and continues its color scheme, based on a rare porcelain teacup owned by a former Emperor of China. The center arbor was created of tapered polished brass and hosted a flutter of lacquered steel butterflies. Clive Minor created this fantasy tree and many other decorative inventions including our famous crystal dragons. Screens and railings were made from a drawing I did of peony blossoms on cracked ice, inspired by a Ming dynasty embroidery (following spread).

My favorite place to dine in the Wynn Las Vegas was at this poolside cabana around the koi pond looking back into the two-story Bartolotta Ristorante di Mare. The grid of twenty-four-inch-diameter polished stainless-steel spheres tethered in the pond gathered the light and the reflection of movements in this busy restaurant, providing guests with a constantly changing animated view. This unexpected installation always elicited a gasp from those descending the sweeping staircase onto the dining level. What's out there? Mystery demands investigation (above). Mystery can be created with unexpected details. The beam ceiling of this restaurant in Las Vegas was swagged with cream-colored backlit taffeta, edged with a glass bead fringe, and scattered with a constellation of eccentric Venetian glass pendant light sources. I found the third-century Roman mosaic of grapes on the fabled Via Margutta in Rome. It is the perfect accessory for a private dining room intended for bacchanalian reveries (right).

The ballrooms and meeting rooms in the Wynn Las Vegas were so successful that we added many more with views of the golf course. During an entire year of European travel, I collected unusual early twentieth-century cabinets and large-scale sculptural accessories. I also commissioned large panels by artist Andrew Fisher. I had no idea what combinations of these elements I would contrive until the days of installations came. I believe that strange and original combinations like these are mystifying, and if I am intrigued by the experience of assembling these combinations, this feeling is transmitted to guests as they move through the halls (opposite and above). We had two-thousand guest rooms in the Wynn Las Vegas. I did not like the superlong registration desk I created at the Bellagio, so for this hotel we created two separate check-in areas. The intimacy of scale was reinforced by the rhythm of mahogany and brass legs on the facade of the desk, and countertop sculptures made of Venetian glass featuring rock-crystal birds and leaves. These details combined to define each area for individual attention and added a sense of "once upon a time." Elaine Wynn allowed us to use a pair of important, large-scale paintings by American artist Miriam Schapiro from her personal collection of work by women artists. They animated the wall with their lively theatrical images and brightly colored fabric collage surfaces (following spread).

Absolutely palatial scale was created with these extra wide and tall hallways for this extraordinary resort, the Wynn Palace Cotai. San Francisco artists Mark Evans and Charley Brown made highly polished panels of flora lifted from an eighteenth-century Chinese porcelain, and the long vista of the hallway was punctuated by a mosaic-topped center table and floral display, which also acted as a locator for the elevators. Large and beautifully decorated spaces are a luxury as long as you know where you are going. While we want to challenge the expectations of our guests, we never want them to be confused or lost. Mystery is not mere confusion (below). This looks exactly like a passage to the casino in Cotai, China, but it is the model we created in Las Vegas. Creating total opulence and grandeur while maintaining an intimate feeling is difficult. We took no chances. This model was fine-tuned over a period of eighteen months to achieve the right balance of beauty and awe (opposite). When I told Steve Wynn I wanted to combine fallen angels with giant Indonesian strangler fig cages, he asked how I came up with these ideas. My answer was simple: "Isn't that what you pay me for?" (The cages are not included in this view, but I collected more than a dozen specimens.) Mark Evans and Charley Brown created these amazing images of falling angels using mirror eglomise, a challenging technique of reverse painting on mirror developed in France. They were tilted into the space at the Lakeside Restaurant Bar in Las Vegas to give a maximum view of your fellow bar mates for the evening, making it easier to find a companion for the fall. They inject a sense of mystery into the room (following spread).

Creating a captivating enticement is the raison d'être of a restaurant entrance. Here, at the Red 8 restaurant in the Encore Boston Harbor, mystery is important as you don't want to "show your hand." Pulling back the curtain, as if it's a hidden space—that creates a sense of tempting mystery and a tingle of anticipation (opposite, top). We created an oval aperture in the ceiling of the ground-floor elevator lobby and in the floor above at the Encore Boston Harbor, then cascaded a collection of red Murano glass chandeliers through the void. The result is completely unexpected—works of exquisite craftmanship that feel a bit like party decorations. The unexpected view both up and down even feels a little bit naughty (opposite, bottom). These few coveted tables at the Red 8 in the Encore Boston Harbor have a casino-side view with the feeling of a sidewalk café in Paris. People-watching, it seems, has always been a human attraction. To accentuate the people watching, we created a hush in the room with draped walls, pulled back like theater curtains to view the constantly changing parade. What is more mysterious than other human beings? Who might pass by next (below)? The company's first floral director, Paige Dixon, was the mentor of legendary floral designer Jeffrey Leatham. She enticed him to join us for every hotel opening celebration. Jeffrey and his Parisian team partnered with hotel floral talents to capture our distinctive color scheme with this abundance of flowers that literally cascades to the floor. It was fortunate that I had three dozen extra-huge golden vases after my complete hotel installation. Jeffrey put them to the very best use, achieving a sense of awe and wonder. An entire pathway of this extravaganza greeted guests on their way to the ballroom for a concert by Andrea Bocelli after a sumptuous dinner at the Wynn Palace Cotai. I felt like I had returned to my Las Vegas roots—dinner and a show (following spread).

NO PLACE LIKE HOME

by Christopher Knight

On one of our first visits to San Miguel de Allende, the exquisite Spanish colonial town on the high plateau known as the Bajío in central Mexico, Roger Thomas was walking down a cobblestone street with some friends and me when, abruptly, he stopped. Across the way, he had spotted something through the open front doors of a modest furniture shop. In a flash he darted inside.

"Fabulous," Roger said, as we followed him in, where his eyes had landed on a simple and lovely dining chair of carved and pieced wood and iron.

This was two decades before the town became an international tourist destination dotted with upscale design boutiques. Everything was guileless and homegrown. San Miguel's legendary charm was evident around every beautiful corner, thanks to government protected status as the 1810 launching pad of the Mexican War of Independence, which blocked modern development in the *centro* that had marred so many other towns. The unassuming store had mostly handmade furniture intended for the dining rooms of local homes, including the chair that Roger zeroed in on.

"¿Tienes más de estas?" Roger asked, availing himself of the translation assistance of another friend, fluent in Spanish, in our party. "Do you have more of these?" The shopkeeper's eyes brightened. "Si!" she replied. "¿Cuantos necesitas? ¿Seis? ¿Ocho? ¿Quizás doce?"

"How many do you need? Six? Eight? Maybe twelve?"

About three thousand, Roger said, the words suddenly needing no translation. The huge number hung in the air. The shopkeeper, stunned, skipped a few beats—then slowly shook her head.

Roger is a hugely successful inventor of the modern genre of resort hotel and casino design, as Louis Daguerre was to the invention of fixed images in photography a hundred years ago, or Hedy Lamarr to the electronic "frequency hopping" for submarine torpedo technology during World War II, which made Wi-Fi communications possible now. The scale of designing for those hotels, especially at a highly competitive place like Las Vegas, where Roger started at it more than four decades ago, is unlike any other design job I know. Three thousand identical side chairs might be needed for the bathroom vanity in every room of the massive lodging, or maybe a coffee shop that would require a stream of potential replacements, or perhaps to accommodate seating in a vast ballroom or convention hall. That mass production was unlikely from the craftsmanship orientation in a rural colonial town in central Mexico was not lost on the designer, but who knows what the possibilities might be?

Roger knows what he likes, and one thing he likes is what he doesn't know—which is to say, a surprise. It was worth asking. Three features of that unconsummated Mexican shopping escapade are relevant to Roger Thomas's specific achievement, beyond the essential issue of negotiating staggering scale. One is an intuitive design sense; it can't be taught—only deepened and refined. The second is an informed historical knowledge, which can only be taught, formally or informally, and is best initiated and absorbed through an alchemical amalgam of obsession and love. And the third—and perhaps most unanticipated yet vitally indispensable—is his work's extraordinary capacity to transform private experience into public spectacle.

No one would mistake the San Miguel side chair for a design by Georges Jacob (1739–1814), *menuisier* and *maître-ebéniste* to King Louis XVI of France, England's Prince of Wales and, after the French Revolution, Emperor Napoleon, and a favorite of Roger's. (Jacob made it through the guillotine-chopped Parisian uprising unscathed, thanks to his close friendship with the revolutionary hero and genius neoclassical painter Jacques-Louis David.) In the unadorned Mexican chair there wasn't any beading, twisted ribbons, guilloches, or fluting to be seen, as there would be in just about every piece of ancien régime furniture in any of the more than two thousand rooms at the Palace of Versailles, elaborated over the course of a few hundred years, or George IV's luxe London residence, Carlton House. The chair just had good proportions, quiet beauty, and comfort.

That it was likely designed and constructed by gifted if modest local artisans had no bearing—positive or negative, either quaintly patronizing or snobbishly supercilious—on Roger's direct response to it as a desirable aesthetic object, or on his curiosity about whether it might somehow be provided in the outsize quantities he required. Roger knows design history inside out. He would know that Jacob, one of the two greatest furniture makers of eighteenth-century France—and one of

the greatest of any-century Europe—was himself far from high-born. *Menuisiers*—joiners, carpenters, woodworkers, and cabinetmakers—were middle-class workers. Jacob, no aristocrat, was born and raised in a peasant family in a small rural commune a hundred miles from the effusively glittering, sometimes menacing court at Versailles. But look what he did!

One easily obscured element needs uncovering in this intersection between the exalted likes of Jacob navigating the halls of aristocratic power and the anonymous craftsmen whose handiwork is encountered in a shop in modern San Miguel de Allende. No shocker, it's this: what both produced is domestic furniture. Not institutional, not corporate—domestic.

Spacious and opulent, Carlton House might not occupy the same social register as a cozy, well-lived stucco-over-rubble-stone house in the Mexican Bajío. But a house is a house. It doesn't matter whether a prince is conducting an audience with ministers in a hall lined with tapestries, or the family is over for a three o'clock *comida* in the kitchen. There's no place like home.

Time and again, what is arresting about Roger Thomas's design work in grand hotels like the Bellagio, Wynn, and Encore in Las Vegas is the way domestic motifs are translated into public venues. Jonah Lehrer, writing in his fascinating profile of Roger in the *New Yorker* a decade ago, notes that at the Wynn, the designer spent two years searching antiques shops from London to Greece to find enough six-foot-tall olive jars from the early twentieth century to decorate the edges of a Wynn grand staircase. Once-ubiquitous storage and shipping containers, they had an original commercial purpose that might have brought them into general proximity of the home. But the very idea of decorating with olive jars, small ones, is what one does in the kitchen, or with larger jars out in the garden at home. Thomas inserted the same idea into another, very different context, expanding the scale from private to public. Familiarity and difference resound against one another, as clear as the timbre produced by a tuning fork, though you can't quite put your finger on what is generating the reverberation.

"I feel like I've seen that before, but I can't quite remember where." The space has an ambience of intimate familiarity, while the public location and grand scale are far beyond the everyday.

The experience happens again and again in spaces Roger's designs, whether large and public like a room filled with gaming tables, a wide corridor lined with luxury boutiques, or your hotel room up on the seventeenth floor. The public lobby lounge of a tower for hotel suites feels more like a luxurious private living room, with a sofa flanked by armchairs cozily positioned around a low coffee table, and a baby grand piano tucked under swagged drapery nearby. The atrium enclosing a baccarat room is like a luminous sunporch at the side of a house that would make an ideal spot for a family get-together, except here it is expanded to monumental scale and elaboration for the purposes of a public venue. The entry table to a restaurant holds

a flower arrangement, a traditional welcoming gesture brightening even a modest foyer at home when the neighbors are expected over for dinner, but here the spatial arrangement is multiplied by eight or a dozen times for overflowing vases. Even a porte cochere for vehicular arrivals might feature elegant urns filled with flowers: welcome home!

Roger of course turns up the luxury dial far beyond what an average person might have at home. Given his impeccable taste level, nothing appears in the slightest out of place. The only thing that's unusual is how unusually beautiful everything is. The piano is lacquered pristine white, the coffee table sports elegant crystal spheres and a pile of oversize art books, the nightstands are mirrored and with beveled edges to shatter the light and make the bed between them sparkle and float. You are home but not home. Which is the point.

Scale is irrespective of a single object's size. Instead, it concerns the ratio of sizes between things. It has an inescapable physical presence, as material as sliding your hand down a handrail carved into a wall or standing next to an antique olive jar taller than a person. But it also has an emotional, psychological quality, which is less often considered. Scale in a contained room or an open architectural environment includes the ratio of that space and its assembled objects to an occupant's memories, experiences, intellect, fantasies, and dreams. Call it psychosocial scale.

In Roger's work, as in every major designer's, that type of scale is distinctive. The ratio here is between an ordinary home, even a lovely one, and an extravagant, even princely one. Furthermore, at a hotel and casino where just about anyone can enter, the experience of that scale is moved from the private sphere into a public one.

The critical flip in Thomas's design work came during the decade between the openings of two Steve Wynn properties, the Mirage (1989) and the Bellagio (1998). Before the Mirage, hotels on the Strip were on a specialty theme kick, whether higher end (Caesars Palace and ancient Rome—1966) or mass market (Circus, Circus, and the Big Top—1968). Like the loosely tropical Mirage, with a risible erupting volcano out front on Las Vegas Boulevard, Treasure Island, which Wynn opened in 1993, had a somewhat more generic fantasy theme—"pirates," identified by the ships in its front yard, complete with booming cannons.

The hotels were themselves public theater. But at the Mirage, the show took a different turn. At the Mirage,

extravagance for its own sake began to overtake any thematic hook. With the Bellagio, it took a leap. Extravagance was tied to the ambience of a house—not just any house, but one that might claim famous pedigrees. The name Bellagio refers to the northern Italian resort village on a promontory jutting out into Lake Como, coveted for its natural beauty. Landmarks include the Villa Melzi, built for an Italian duke instrumental in the country's nineteenth-century unification, and Villa Serbelloni and its park, an eighteenth-century terraced garden with lake views, the house dating to the sixteenth century and now a scholars and artists retreat for the Rockefeller Foundation. The villas are splendid and impressive palaces, which is another way of saying they began their historic lives as private homes.

A hotel visitor didn't need to know these details. Domestic extravagance could be said to be the nominal "theme" of Roger's Bellagio, but it is mostly sensed. Outdoors, the building's architects designed a faux village clustered on the shore of an artificial lake, its preprogrammed "dancing waters" a thoroughly abstract fountain. The hotel's big, thirty-six-story curved facade behind the lakeside village opens wide, its arc partly a showman's ta-da! and partly an inviting hug. Inside, it was Roger Thomas World. There, the psychosocial scale is: every man a duke, every woman a duchess, spending leisure time at the family's sumptuous country villa.

Later, at the Wynn Las Vegas (2005) and the adjacent Encore Las Vegas (2008), even the Bellagio's loose thematic attachments were dropped. There are plenty of interior design flourishes that might be traced to the House of Habsburg or Imperial China, but all are filtered through Roger's own design sensibility, voluminously elaborated. (I don't recall ever seeing Roger without a small sketchbook in his pocket or bag, not for use to immediately record a cornice detail or a flowering tree that he is looking at in real time, but to quickly capture recollections of ones he has seen in the past that have lodged in his memory and demand escape. The sketches become design sourcebooks.) "I don't do focus groups," he also told the *New Yorker*'s Lehrer of his design process. "I create rooms I want to be in." His past creates a visionary future unfurling in the present.

Paradoxical as it may seem, the domestic core of these otherwise lavish public spaces demands credit as the beating heart of their social success. The designer's highly refined, deeply informed aesthetics of personal living, unexpected in a commercial setting, are pumped up to the dazzling level of public spectacle.

Roger, with his husband, Arthur Libera, a licensing agent and business partner, has long partaken of gay men's enthusiastic reverence for creating house and home. For a society historically uncomfortable with homosexuality, the home is a doubly charged environment. It is first an intimate place where youthful alienation, estrangement, and disaffection are most sorely experienced. Then, as its potential as a place of adult refuge from a hostile world is intuited, creating a new home both confident and distinctive becomes a common fixation. In the home away from home that is the purpose and meaning of a hotel and resort, the domestic language of Roger Thomas's work has been an inspiration for transformative design. An internalized sense of "home" is enlarged and complicated for often grand, sometimes playful, always magnificent public display.

BUSHWHACKED
Paris + Venice   Mar 2020

INSPIRATION BEGINS AT HOME

by Roger Thomas

I want my hotel guests to live as well as I do. That said, my hotel designs do not resemble my homes. They do not share a style, aesthetic, or scale. The reason is simply that my homes incorporate my personal collections—an assembly of treasured objects I have discovered in my travels or acquired from artists I have known.

The criterion for personal acquisition is total enchantment. It begins with attraction—the object must catch the eye—but it goes far beyond that. I seek out objects that ultimately present a series of questions that might take a long time to consider and may never be answered; they are ripe with mystery. These are usually objects that challenge my sense of design and my expectations of the possible. They expand the boundaries of my understanding, both of design and design history. The furniture selected must also fit my criteria for total comfort, as I believe that this is an essential criterion for well-designed objects. Form without function is not acceptable.

However, my hotel designs do reflect everything I have learned from my homes. I use my residential spaces as a laboratory to test ideas, and I apply this knowledge to all my design projects. The laboratory part comes in the placement of the objects. I never buy pieces for specific locations. When they arrive, I look for opportunities to animate a space or to place something exactly where it should not be in order to create surprise, tension, or contrast. Then, I continue to move objects from place to place on a regular basis as an experiment in relationships. Looking for these new relationships teaches me to always remain open to opportunities and possibility.

My Las Vegas and California homes have a movable hanging system for art so that it can be changed on a regular basis. Art that remains in place for a long time often becomes the wall cover. It becomes such an expected part of the

room that it ceases to be appreciated on its own or considered for close inspection—two crucial elements that keep art alive. It's not enough to look—we must see.

I also constantly experiment with solutions for new challenges at home. Digital media and portable platforms, the discovery of new materials, or the sad announcements of a familiar material becoming extinct—these all lead me to seek out novel solutions, which I first test out in my private spaces.

And then there's the urgent need to create sustainable designs. My homes have often been the proving ground for potential answers to this challenge. Epoxy fortified flooring, washable paint, and durable eco-friendly textiles have all been put to the personal test first. Before we roll them out at the hotels, I want to make sure the ecological substitute is not a sacrifice.

There is no such thing as a perfect room—design is a never-ending process. My homes are a testament to that relentless need to keep solving problems in ways that are creative, considerate, and kind. Tomorrow, I will probably rearrange the items on my coffee table, or change the art in my bedroom, or search for a new fabric for my dining chairs.

What I learn here, at home, inspires my solutions at work. That's because living with a design is the ultimate test. Does it last? Is it comfortable? Does it keep surprising me?

ADDITIONAL CAPTION INFORMATION

Front cover: Wynn Encore Las Vegas Baccarat Private Salon. Inspired by a favorite artist, James Abbott McNeill Whistler, my friends at Fromental, London, created these marvelous peacock panels in hand-painted and hand-stitched fine Chinese silk. I wanted a dramatic entrance to suggest the opulence beyond.

Back cover: Wynn Las Vegas Wing Lei Restaurant. The model for this heroically scaled dragon was a fine wood object, only three inches high, that I found in Hong Kong. The sphere it holds is solid rare onyx. Centered between two-hundred-year-old pomegranate trees, this tableau becomes the focus of the entire restaurant.

Endpaper spread, front: Wynn Encore Las Vegas XS Nightclub Entry. I decided to celebrate beautiful bodies in this nightspot. Isn't that why we go to nightclubs? This deep relief was created by scanning live models, printing those scans in three dimensions, and then arranging them under plaster-laden stretch fabric while suspended from the ceiling. The surface was covered with gold leaf over a red ground.

Endpaper spread, back: Wynn Palace Cotai Ballroom Corridor. During the hotel's grand opening, unique and elaborate floral designs by Jeffrey Latham graced this path to the ballroom—making it truly ready for celebration.

Page 9: Encore Las Vegas Lobby, 2008.

Page 10: The oculus in Roger Thomas's Las Vegas home, designed by architect Mark Mack.

Page 12: Roger Thomas's birthday celebration with his parents and older brother, Peter, at the Sands Hotel and Casino, Las Vegas, 1959.

Page 13: Roger with his father, E. Parry Thomas, 1975.

Page 14, top: E. Parry Thomas and Steve Wynn with the Lifetime Achievement Award at the American Academy, 1996.

Page 14, bottom: Roger and Janellen Radoff, 2005.

Page 15, top: Guests gambling at the Dunes Hotel Casino, Las Vegas, 1956.

Page 15, bottom: The Mirage Hotel and Casino, Las Vegas, 1989.

Page 16, top: Roy Horn, Roger Thomas, and Siegfried Fischbacher at the Jungle Palace, Las Vegas, early 1990s.

Page 16, middle: The Battle of Buccaneer Bay: cannons fire, pyrotechnics explode, and stuntmen are thrown into the waters as the British Royal Navy challenges the pirates in a battle to the finish at Treasure Island, Las Vegas, 1993.

Page 16, bottom: Andy Warhol taking a polaroid of Roger Thomas for his portrait in 1981.

Page 17: A capriccio pen and ink drawing by Roger Thomas, 2021.

Page 18: Fiori di Como by Dale Chihuly in the Bellagio Guest Reception, Las Vegas, 1998.

Page 19: A George Jacob armchair, ca. 1780–1785.

Pages 20–21: Hotel guests are enchanted by the ballet of live jellyfish in this monumental aquarium at the Encore Macau's reception area. The desk front is a basket-weave pattern of cast glass over gold tea paper, inspired by the work of René Lalique. The custom drapery fabric is by Opuzen, and the largest bespoke tassels are tied upward to maintain the romantic curve of the pleated fabric. The mango linen wall upholstery throughout the hotel is trimmed with fuchsia ribbon from Samuel & Sons.

Page 248: A humble Mexican chair, late eighteenth century.

Page 249, top: The one- to three-hundred-year-old urns showcased at Bartolotta Ristorante di Mare at the Wynn Las Vegas, 2005, hail from around the world.

Page 249, bottom: A cast and beaded glass peacock by Clive Miner at the Encore Las Vegas atrium garden, 2008.

Page 250, top: An aerial view of the Sands Hotel and Casino looking north up the Las Vegas Strip, 1975.

Page 250, bottom: The Encore, Wynn and Wynn Golf Club are visible in this aerial view of the Las Vegas Strip looking south, 2017.

Page 251: A capriccio pen and ink drawing by Roger Thomas, 2020.

Page 252: The salon of our apartment in Venice has a particularly beautiful original Terrazzo floor, which inspired its tonality. The walls are covered in a Benjamin Moore paint in exactly the color of the Grand Canal at 2:30 pm in the afternoon. The Louis XVI chairs were made in Paris by George Jacob in ca. 1780–1785, and the sixteenth-century painting of San Sebastian is by Venetian artist Giovanni Contarini.

Page 253, top left: The cast-concrete sculpture by Roger Thomas for Trevi is in front of our Las Vegas home's pool, 2003.

Page 253, top right: A view in front of a moving wall in the library of our Las Vegas home, designed by architect Mark Mack, showing an assemblage of treasured objects: a still life by Giorgio Morandi, an eighteenth-century Venetian chair brought into the twenty-first century with cobalt blue leather, a 1920s table made in Yellowstone National Park, and a two-man wedding cake topper created by Ruth Marten.

Page 253, bottom: The library in our Marin County, California, home, 2020.

ACKNOWLEDGMENTS

I was asked in an interview during the opening of the Wynn Las Vegas Resort in 2005, "How long did it take to design the project?" My answer was fifty-four years. Everything I've done has reflected a lifetime before and has depended on the contributions of countless individuals and meaningful encounters. I am grateful for all of them.

It started with my parents who gave perhaps the greatest gift I have ever received. They encouraged me to do what I truly loved. It was also my parents who introduced me to Steve and Elaine Wynn. Without Steve and Elaine Wynn absolutely nothing in this book would have been possible. For their patronage, their encouragement, and the many lessons they have taught me I am forever indebted. Nothing I created could have happened without their ideas and their demands that I accomplish more than I thought possible. None of this extravagance would have been possible without the leadership of my father, Parry Thomas, and his partner, Jerry Mack, who activated the financial machine of Las Vegas and paved the way for publicly owned corporate ownership of resort casino hotels.

During my entire career, I have been blessed with a studio filled with an extraordinary team of talented and dedicated professionals. It is always a risk to name names, but I feel compelled. My design partner of over twenty years, Janellen Radoff, was the most talented colorist and a persistent instigator of inspiration. I miss her talents, her wit, and her wisdom. Architect DeRuyter Butler is absolutely the best creator of the hotel resort machine and a generous and kind collaborator. Karina Ashworth managed the studio and the production and made these projects happen. Todd-Avery Lenahan is a valued colleague, a great creator, and a source of wonderful ideas; he is now my successor. Thanks to Alex Woogmaster, protégé and partner on many of these spaces. Alex revived my career and got me to the finish line. I am deeply indebted to all the artists and craftsmen who contributed to the realities of these projects. Thank you for inventing and making the seemingly impossible possible.

My friend Russell MacMasters beautifully captured the first thirty years of my career with his distinctive lens. Barbara Kraft and Roger Davies have continued to record my work with their own singular views. Together, they are responsible for the inspired images on these pages.

Jonah Lehrer is responsible for so much, including making me sound smarter than I am, and my dear friends Cindy Allen and Christopher Knight responded to my call and contributed original and provocative thoughts, as they have throughout my career.

Creating this book has been a challenge as well as a labor of love. This would not have been accomplished without the navigation and guidance of my agents, Cherie Bustamante and Andrea Monfried, the careful structure and clear constructive critiques of my editor, Sandra Gilbert Freidus, and the constant support of my friend and longtime collaborator Cherie Flannigan. If you love the look and design of this book as much as I do, then we must all thank the genius of Matthew Kraus and Sam Shahid, whose extraordinary talents grace these pages cover to cover.

Dear friends Penny Drue Baird, Timothy Corrigan, and Vicente Wolf were generous in sharing their considerable experiences with creating a book on design. This book would not exist without the instigation and support of my extraordinary husband, Arthur Libera. And finally, to my daughter, Drew Thomas. I pass this torch into your talented hands.

All photography courtesy of Wynn Resorts Archives (unless otherwise specified), taken by the following photographers:

Barbara Kraft: front and back jacket; endpapers; pages 9; 14, bottom; 20–21; 22; 24–25; 26, top and bottom; 27; 28–29; 32–33; 34; 35; 36–37; 38; 39; 40–41; 42; 46; 47, top and bottom; 48; 49; 50–51; 52; 53; 54; 55; 56–57; 60–61; 62; 64–65; 66; 67; 68, top and bottom; 69; 70–71; 72, top and bottom; 74–75; 76; 78–79; 86–87; 88; 89; 90; 91, top and bottom; 92–93; 94; 95; 96; 97, top and bottom; 98–99; 100; 101; 102; 103, top and bottom; 104–05; 108; 109; 110–11; 116–17; 118; 120–21; 122; 126; 127; 128–29; 130; 131; 132; 133, top and bottom; 138; 139; 140–41; 142, top and bottom; 143; 148–49; 150; 151; 152–53; 154; 155; 156–57; 158, top and bottom; 159; 160–61; 162; 163; 164–65; 166; 167; 168–69; 174; 176–77; 180–81; 182; 183; 184–85; 186; 187; 188–89; 190; 192; 193; 194–95; 196; 198–99; 200; 202–03; 204; 205; 207; 210; 211; 212; 213; 214–15; 217; 218; 219; 222; 227; 234; 235; 236, top and bottom; 237; 238–39; 240; 241; 242–43; 244, top and bottom; 245; 249, top.

Francis George: pages 84; 249, bottom.

Roger Davies: pages 30; 31, top and bottom; 52; 58; 59; 73; 77; 80; 81; 82–83; 106; 107; 112; 113, top and bottom; 114; 115; 124–25; 136; 137; 144–45; 146; 172–73; 178; 179, top and bottom; 197, top; 206; 208–09; 216, top and bottom; 220–21; 224–25; 232–33; 246–47.

Russell MacMasters: pages 43; 44–45; 123; 134–35; 170; 171; 191; 197, bottom; 226; 228–29; 230; 231.

Additional Photography Credits:

Benedetta Pignatelli: pages 10; 253, top left and right. **Collection of Lari Pittman and Roy Dowell:** page 248. **Jean-François Jaussaud:** page 252. **Las Vegas News Bureau Collection, LVCVA Archive:** pages 15, top, July 2, 1956; 250, top. **Roger Davies:** page 253, bottom. **Roger P. Thomas Personal Archive:** pages 14, bottom, photograph by Barbara Kraft; 17; 18, photograph by Russell MacMasters; 251; jacket flap, photograph by Francis George. **Sam Morris/Las Vegas News Bureau Collection:** page 250, bottom, August 2, 2017. **Siegfried and Roy Archive:** page 16, top. **Stephen Molasky:** page 16, bottom. **The Metropolitan Museum of Art, New York, Archive:** page 19. **The Neon Museum Las Vegas Archive:** photographs by Russell MacMasters: pages 15, bottom; 16, middle. **Thomas Family Archive:** pages 12; 13; 14, top.

Book Design: Sam Shahid & Matthew Kraus, Shahid / Kraus & Company

First published in the United States of America in 2024 by
Rizzoli International Publications, Inc.
300 Park Avenue South
New York, NY 10010
www.rizzoliusa.com

© 2024 Roger Thomas

Publisher: Charles Miers
Editor: Sandra Gilbert Freidus
Editorial Assistance: Hilary Ney, Kelli Rae Patton, and Rachel Selekman
Design Assistance: Olivia Russin
Production Manager: Alyn Evans
Managing Editor: Lynn Scrabis

Printed in Hong Kong

ISBN 13: 978-0-8478-9995-1

Library of Congress Control Number: 2023948321

Visit us online:
Facebook.com/RizzoliNewYork
instagram.com/rizzolibooks
twitter.com/Rizzoli_Books
pinterest.com/rizzolibooks
youtube.com/user/RizzoliNY
issuu.com/Rizzoli